andy**warhol**

prince**of**pop

andy**warhol**

princeof**pop**

jan greenberg & sandra jordan

delacorte press

Published by
Delacorte Press
an imprint of
Random House Children's Books
a division of Random House, Inc.
New York

Visit us on the Web! www.randomhouse.com/teens
Educators and librarians, for a variety of teaching tools, visit us at
www.randomhouse.com/teachers

Library of Congress Cataloging-in-Publication Data is available upon request.
ISBN 0-385-73056-X (trade) — ISBN 0-385-90079-1 (GLB)

The text of this book is set in 12-point Helvetica 45 Light.

Book design by Kenneth Holcomb

Printed in the United States of America

October 2004

10   9   8   7   6   5   4   3   2   1

BVG

for

beverlyhorowitz
and
françoise**bui**

who make it all happen

contents

Pittsburgh Days, 1928–1940   1

Genuine as a Fingerprint, 1941–1945   11

Why Pick on Me?, 1945–1949   16

Warhola to Warhol, 1950–1951   22

Making It, 1952–1959   28

Pop!, 1960–1961   37

Soup Cans and Celebrities, 1962   43

Fame!, 1963   52

Made in America, 1963–1964   60

The Swinging Silver Factory, 1964   66

The Prince of Pop, 1964   72

Poor Little Rich Girl, 1965   80

The Velvet Underground, 1966   86

Chelsea Girls, 1966   91

Enter Fred Hughes, 1967   95

Shot!, 1968   100

Interview, 1969–1970   107

Putting My Andy On, 1970–1974   114

Andy Warhol Enterprises, 1975–1982   121

The Last Years, 1982–1987   125

Postscript   134

Some Important Dates   139

Selected Films by Andy Warhol   147

Books by Andy Warhol   149

Glossary of Artists and Art Terms   150

Notes   158

Sources   181

Photography Credits   183

Index   185

andy**warhol**

prince**of**pop

Pittsburgh Days 1928–1940

I never wanted to be a painter. I wanted to be a tap dancer. —Andy Warhol

He loved her. Entranced, he sat in the darkened movie theater while child star Shirley Temple tap-danced her way into his heart. In *Poor Little Rich Girl,* the silver-screen charmer with the adorable dimples and fifty-six golden curls triumphed over adversity with a smile. In Andy's world, work was grueling, but Shirley made it look like fun. He stored away impressions of his idol to imitate later on. For now, Andy worshipped Shirley from afar, even sending off a dime to join her fan club. The photograph that came in the mail was signed "To Andrew Warhola, from Shirley Temple." Carefully placed in a scrapbook, it would remain one of Andy's treasured possessions. This marked the beginning of his lasting passion for celebrities, collecting their autographs and photos, creating a fantasy life that would determine his future.

Both were eight years old, born in 1928, but how different Shirley's life was from Andy's. He could dream about being a Hollywood star; life in Pittsburgh offered a grimmer picture. "Being born," Andy later said, "is like being kidnapped. And then sold into slavery."

Andy came into the world in the back bedroom of his family's tiny apartment at 73 Orr Street in Pittsburgh's grimy immigrant ghetto. Shortly after his birth, his father, Andrej Warhola, lost his construction job, and the family moved to an even more cramped two-room apartment. Andy shared a bed with his older brothers, Paul and John. The bathtub sat in the middle of the kitchen—convenient because with the apartment's primitive plumbing, anyone wanting hot water had to heat it on the stove. In the alley behind the building was a communal privy.

The precocious Andy walked and talked early, and it was clear to everyone that he was bright, if a bit of a handful. His blond, cherubic looks were a contrast to those of his more robust brothers, and his mother, Julia, deciding her youngest child's health was delicate, coddled him. Although they didn't own a radio (and commercial television didn't exist), they found ways to entertain themselves. When the boys' games grew too rambunctious for the family's close quarters, Julia brought them into the kitchen, gave them paper and crayons, and announced a contest for the best drawing. Julia was artistic, and all three Warhola boys inherited some of her gift, but Andy easily outstripped his brothers. He might have been the youngest, but he always won the giant Hershey bar Julia offered as a prize.

From the beginning, making art was what Andy liked to do best. His brother John remembered a neighborhood baseball game where Andy reluctantly took a position in the outfield.

"Someone hit a baseball where Andy was supposed to be, and Andy wasn't there. I later found him sitting in front of the house drawing flowers. Andy never argued, he never swore, he didn't go in for rough stuff. I always thought he was going to be a priest."

Andy isn't known to have considered that possibility, but he dutifully attended church with Julia during the week as well as on Sunday. The Byzantine Catholic Church loomed large in the devout Warhola family. From their apartment they walked three miles down a winding road and across the railroad tracks to St. John Chrysostom. "Rain or shine, there were no excuses," John recalled. The priest sat all the boys—including Andy—in the first row, where they at least had to pretend to pay attention during the long service. At the altar stood a golden screen, closely hung with square upon square, row upon row of icons—sacred paintings of saints. These repetitive images would have a profound effect on Andy's art.

Their father insisted that Sunday be strictly observed, but John remembered it as a joyous time, mainly because of Julia's influence. "My mother . . . liked going to church better than material things. She never believed in being wealthy—she believed just being a real good person made you happy. We were taught never to hurt anybody, to believe you're just here for a short time and you're going to leave the material things behind."

There weren't many material things to leave. Andy's family originated in Carpatho-Ruthenia, a poor farming area of the Carpathian Mountains that was passed back and forth in the constant wars and border disputes among Czechoslovakia, Ukraine, and Hungary. Andrej and Julia Warhola—along with

3

many members of both of their families—came to America seeking work and a better life.

The Pittsburgh where the Warholas settled was a far different town in the 1920s and 1930s than it is today. Located at the point where three rivers meet, it was the bustling steel-making capital of America. Iron ore arrived from vast strip mines in northern Minnesota, coal from Pennsylvania. Even when unemployment was high during the Great Depression of the thirties, and labor protesters and private policemen fought in the streets of the city, the steel mills roared twenty-four hours a day, filling the daytime sky with so much smoke that drivers had to keep their headlights on. The word *smog* was invented to describe the sooty air that hung over Pittsburgh. At night the Bessemer converters in the steel mills lit up the sky like fireworks, and small trains left the mills and dumped the hot, glowing slag on the hillsides, where it cascaded down in burning rivulets.

Many other groups of Middle Europeans populated the neighborhood called Soho, where the Warhola family lived. They all had been lured there by the promise of America, the land of golden opportunity; instead they found backbreaking, often dangerous jobs that paid meager wages. The cheaply built housing that was all they could afford sometimes lacked even the basics of heat, hot water, and safe sanitation. Disease was a constant threat. Nobody seemed to care. The immigrants were treated as interlopers in their adopted country, despised for their imperfect English, their strange customs, and most of all for their poverty.

However, in several respects Andy was fortunate. His father managed to keep food on the table and a roof over their heads during the toughest years of the Depression. He labored six days a week, twelve hours a day, taking odd jobs when he was laid off from construction work. Sundays were spent in church. After the long service, the Warholas visited the various aunts, uncles, and cousins who also had moved to the Pittsburgh area. Unlike many of his fellows, Andrej saved his money and did not drink or gamble to relieve the stress of his unremitting drudgery. His critics, some of them within the family, went so far as to call him a tightfisted workaholic. Andy inherited both his father's capacity for hard work and his thrifty nature.

In contrast to Andrej, whose stern glance compelled instant obedience from his sons, Julia was warmhearted and loving. John said, "She could really make you laugh." She told rambling, mythic stories about the "old country" in Po Nasemu, the Carpo-Rusyn language, a mixture of Hungarian and Ukrainian, that all the Warholas spoke at home. She also loved to sing, and enjoyed regaling her listeners with stories of the year when she and one of her sisters had traveled around the Ruthenian countryside singing with the Gypsies.

It was just after Julia's Gypsy singing tour that she encountered the handsome, wavy-haired Andrej, who had worked for several years in America before returning home to find a suitable bride. They married in a festive village wedding that lasted for days. Three years later, Europe was on the brink of war, and Julia was pregnant with their first child. Andrej returned to America alone, fearing that otherwise he would be drafted into the Austrian army. When he was settled with a job and a place to live he would send for Julia and the baby. Shortly after his departure, Julia gave birth to a daughter who survived only a few weeks, probably because no medical treatment was available. The death plunged Julia into despair, but there was no way she could reach Andrej to share her grief. World War I had begun, and several warring armies made travel between Carpatho-Ruthenia and America too dangerous. It would be nine years before Julia finally joined Andrej in Pittsburgh. There she had three more children, Paul in 1922, John in 1925, and Andy, the last, in 1928.

The older boys assumed a somewhat paternal attitude toward their baby brother, as Andrej's work often took him out of town during the week. Paul thought that shy Andy, who hid behind his doting mother's skirts when visitors came to the house, was becoming a sissy and needed discipline. He dragged his crying four-year-old sibling off to school and enrolled him in the first grade. Andy lasted barely a day. After a little girl hit him, he went home in tears, refusing to go back. Julia said, "Don't push him. He's too young yet." For two more years Andy happily stayed home with his mother.

During that time the Warholas moved, and by some bureaucratic error, Holmes Elementary School in their new neighborhood counted Andy's single day in first grade as a full year. He was placed in the second grade. Because his family conversed in Po Nasemu, he spoke broken English, but he easily caught up with his classmates, and his unusual talent for drawing was quickly noticed. "He was a good little artist in second grade," one of his teachers recalled. In fact, all his teachers throughout the years seemed to recognize his art ability. Probably because he preferred crayons to baseball bats, most of Andy's friends in grade school were girls. According to Margie Girman and Mina Serbin, his best friends at Holmes, girls liked to be around Andy, who was good company and flattered them with his attention.

At age seven he surprised his parents by requesting his own movie projector, a rather exotic item for an ordinary household. John said, "My dad couldn't afford to buy it, so my mother would do some housework one or two days a

week. . . . She saved the money up and got it for Andy."
Andy spent every nickel he scrounged by running errands
and selling newspapers to buy films of Mickey Mouse and
other cartoons. The family didn't bother with a screen; he
projected the films over and over on a bare wall, and then he
drew his own copies.

Andy was eight when all Julia's fears about his health
came true. He caught rheumatic fever, a disease that in the
days before penicillin could leave a child with a weak heart or
crippling arthritis—if it didn't kill him. The only treatment available was bed rest. After a month's absence from school Andy
was told it was time to go back to class. No one paid attention to his pleas that he still felt sick; everyone in the family,
except Julia, thought he was a crybaby. With their father
away, Paul enlisted a burly next-door neighbor to carry his
kicking and shrieking brother down the street to Holmes
Elementary.

Before the fever Andy's shyness and creative tempera-
ment had made him a teacher's pet, but now school became
a torment. His hands shook so badly he could not write on
the blackboard; his knees buckled when he walked. The
other students mocked his disabilities. Eventually the family
doctor diagnosed the condition as chorea, a complication of
rheumatic fever that is also known as St. Vitus' dance, because those who have it shake uncontrollably. Again the only
available treatment was bed rest. Later, when Andy talked
about this period of his life, he referred to his illness as a series of nervous breakdowns, yet in some ways it seems to
have provided the happiest months of his childhood. Under
the doting gaze of his mother, he lay in bed with his comics

and coloring books, drifting and dreaming, free to contemplate and fantasize. He definitely preferred staying home.

Thanks to Andrej's frugal ways, the family recently had purchased a house on Dawson Street in the more middle-class neighborhood of Oakland. For the first time they had the luxury of an indoor bathroom with hot and cold running water, and a furnace in the cellar for central heating. There were two bedrooms, a living room, a separate dining room, and an attic, which Paul renovated into a third bedroom for himself.

Julia now moved her ailing son's bed into the dining room. She put the family's only radio there and showered Andy with devoted care. When he finished a page in his coloring book, Julia gave him one of the Hershey bars she used to reward good behavior. Sometimes, at his pleading, she read his comic books aloud to him. Her accent in English often was incomprehensible even to her son, but he enjoyed the attention and didn't tell her. Paul, perhaps feeling guilty about his part in sending Andy back to school prematurely, also spent extra time with his baby brother, showing him how to use wax to transfer a comic strip onto another piece of paper. Andy's illness cemented once and for all his status as a special child who needed to be protected. Far from resenting him, his two older brothers looked out for him, and when they weren't around, they asked their friends to keep an eye on him.

Once Andy finally returned to school, his long absence didn't affect his grades. The next year, his teacher recommended him for a gifted children's class given free on Saturday mornings at the Carnegie Institute. Students from all over the city attended. Not only could Andy see great art and improve his drawing skills, but he also was exposed to children from Pittsburgh's upper class. They arrived in gleaming automobiles, escorted by mothers dressed in expensively tailored suits and fur coats. The movies Andy loved showed Hollywood's version of glittering extravagance, but now, on Saturday mornings at the museum, he gained a close-up view of an affluent and privileged way of life that looked out of reach for a Ruthenian boy from a blue-collar family.

Still, in art classes all the children had an equal chance. Three hundred budding artists sat together in long rows, balancing Masonite drawing boards on their laps while they drew with crayons. Andy quickly stood out. The teacher, Joseph Fitzpatrick, recalled that socially Andy had no manners or consideration for others, but artistically he was both accomplished and individualistic. "From the class every week I had what they called an honor roll," Fitzpatrick said, "and people who were on the honor roll [stood] at easels on the stage. . . . Andy was up on the stage in the honor roll many times."

But Saturday classes and art in school were not enough to satisfy Andy. With a grade-school friend, Nick Kish, who also liked to draw, Andy used to sneak upstairs to Nick's parents' room. Together they sat in front of a very large mirror and drew self-portraits. Nick said, "We used to show ourselves the way [we thought] others saw us, and [the results] were horrible. We didn't think too much of ourselves. Andy's self-portraits were always very white because his skin was so fair. In fact, in one of them he took chalk and put it over his face in the drawing, at which point both of us burst out laughing because it looked like death warmed over." A remarkable portrait Andy drew of Nick demonstrated the unusual skill he had already developed.

Andy spent four defining years in Joseph Fitzpatrick's class. The dedicated teacher tried to impart more than

9

technical skills to his students. Fitzpatrick paced back and forth on the stage, lecturing them: "Art is not just a subject. It's a way of life. It's the only subject you use from the time you open your eyes in the morning until you close them at night. Everything you look at has art or the lack of art." Andy would internalize Fitzpatrick's lesson, that art was everywhere you looked, in ways his teacher never imagined.

Genuine as a Fingerprint   1941–1945

I tried and tried when I was younger to learn something about love, and since it wasn't taught in school I turned to the movies for some clues about what love is and what to do about it. —Andy Warhol

For three days the body of Andrej Warhola was laid out in the living room of the small house on Dawson Street. This was the custom of their church, but the thought of sleeping in his bedroom while his dead father lay downstairs was more than the traumatized thirteen-year-old Andy could stand. He hid under the bed and wouldn't come out, begging to stay with his aunt Mary and cousin Tinka until after the funeral. Julia, fearing that Andy's grief would trigger a relapse of his St. Vitus' dance, let him go. He came home for the service, but the experience left Andy with an abiding fear of death. In the future, he hardly ever attended funerals, quipping that death was too abstract. He preferred pretending that people who died had just gone shopping.

Andy later gave different versions of Andrej's death to

interviewers, often saying his father had been killed in a coal mining accident. Actually, Andrej, who had already suffered from jaundice, caught hepatitis while working on one of his construction jobs away from home. He probably died of peritonitis. Julia had pleaded with her husband not to go, thinking that now that they had a little cash in the bank, he could afford to turn down dangerous assignments. However, Andrej wasn't one to pass up any chance to earn money. He was planning for his family's future. Paul and John were strong and steady, hard workers if not scholastically gifted. They would be all right. But he also believed that his youngest son had talent, and he had made an important decision. Andy would go to college.

When Andrej realized he was dying, he asked Paul and John to look after their mother and little brother. Julia wasn't good with finances, so he wanted to ensure that the post office savings bonds he had earmarked for Andy's education would be used that way. Paul and John promised to honor his wish.

With Andrej's death, poverty squeezed the family tighter than ever. Paul took over as the main support, but he was engaged to be married, and a new wife would stretch his finances. After the attack on Pearl Harbor on December 7, 1941, America entered World War II, and Paul was sent to fight overseas, leaving only John to look after his mother, brother, and now pregnant sister-in-law. It would be up to him to see that Andrej's dying requests were carried out.

Puberty hit the still grieving Andy hard. His skin, already pale and blotchy from his bout with St. Vitus' dance, broke out in fiery acne, including a nose so swollen and inflamed that his family teased him with the nickname Andy the Red-Nosed Warhola. The change in his appearance didn't help

Andy's shaky self-confidence. People who knew him in high school said he was quiet and odd-looking, but dressed like the rest in a pullover and saddle shoes. After school he often went to the local drugstore hangout, Yohe's. There he sat in a booth and drew people, using his artistic gift as a way to win a measure of acceptance.

He also continued to draw with Nick Kish and remained close with Margie Girman and Mina Serbin. Mina said, "I was captain of the cheerleaders and I was popular, but I wasn't that pretty. [Andy] would always say how beautiful my hair was or what nice colors I was wearing. We didn't really have dates in those days . . . but we went bowling . . . together and we went ice-skating, and we'd walk to the movies holding hands." By Andy's junior year he was on the student board of the high school canteen, where kids went to drink Cokes and dance.

No matter how it seemed to those around him, Andy felt like an outsider. "I wasn't amazingly popular, but I had some nice friends. I wasn't very close to anyone, although I guess I wanted to be, because when I would see the kids telling one another their problems, I felt left out. No one confided in me—I wasn't the type they wanted to confide in, I guess."

Some of this feeling might have come from his family situation. The child of immigrant parents, Andy's home life was different from that of more assimilated families in his neighborhood. But he also must have suspected deeper problems. While he liked girls and counted them among his closest friends, he showed no signs of being attracted to them the way other boys were. Yet to whom could he talk about his feelings? In Pittsburgh in the early forties, high school students' information about sex was limited to prohibitions against having it. Sexuality was represented as strictly the

13

province of adult married couples. The subject of homosexuality was taboo, considered shameful, not as a legitimate sexual preference. In many states homosexual acts were illegal. And most psychiatrists believed that it was a pathology that could be "cured" by the right treatment.

The world of the movies, which Andy worshipped, would have been no more help than his friends and family. Films hinted at gayness by ridiculing effeminate behavior. Andy was definitely effeminate. Many of his mannerisms—the way he walked, clasped his hands under his chin, or tilted his head—seemed to have been influenced by his crush on Shirley Temple. In spite of this, no one suspected him of being gay. A male friend from high school said, "It wasn't the sort of thing one thought about at the time." Andy never spoke directly about any conflicts regarding his sexual identity, although he later wrote that he always knew he would never get married or have children. "I didn't want them to have the same problems I did. I don't think anybody deserves it."

Losing his father was hard enough for Andy, but in the fall of 1944, at the beginning of his senior year, Julia was diagnosed with colon cancer. The doctors said that her only chance was a risky new operation called a colostomy. Andy was worried that his mother would die, and his grades skidded. For the first time in high school he didn't take an art class. Julia survived the operation, but her convalescence took almost a year. John arranged his work hours so that he cared for Julia during the day, and Andy took over after school.

Julia needed his help for now, but there was no question that Andy was headed for college. In spite of his drop in grades, two prestigious local universities with excellent art programs, the University of Pittsburgh (Pitt) and the Carnegie

Institute of Technology (Carnegie Tech), accepted him. He planned to go to Pitt, where his friend Nick Kish also had applied, but at the last minute Nick was drafted. Andy, whose seventeenth birthday occurred only a few weeks before the beginning of his freshman year, was too young for the draft, but he worried about getting lost in the crowd at Pitt. Instead he chose the smaller Carnegie Tech. In October of 1945 he would start a new life, not far from his house, but worlds away from Dawson Street.

Why Pick on Me?   1945–1949

Artists are never intellectuals, that's why they're artists. —Andy Warhol

Carnegie Tech called the process judgment, and for some, including Andy, it was Judgment Day. Artworks from the freshman class hung alphabetically down a long wall. With World War II recently over, the class had been warned that fifteen students would be dropped to make room for the returning veterans who had applied for admission. Slowly the faculty members moved down the hall, assigning grades for the semester. At last they came to the *W*s—Andy Warhola's freshman work. "He's not going to fit," announced one of the instructors. Andy was out.

Upon hearing the bad news, Andy did what any sensitive seventeen-year-old boy would do: "I created a big scene and cried." Carnegie Tech was a top school, not only in Pittsburgh but nationally, and a number of well-known artists taught there. They were tough, talented, and professional, but they didn't always know what to make of Andy Warhola. Philip Pearlstein, an older student who would succeed later as a painter, said, "It was very apparent to all of the students that Andy was extraordinarily talented. It was not apparent to the faculty."

Throughout his first year Andy regularly split the faculty down the middle between those who thought he was without talent and those who liked his work. Even some of the latter didn't think he had much of a future. One of his teachers said, "If anyone would have asked me who was least likely to succeed, I would have said Andy Warhola."

Russell Hyde, a teacher known to the students as Papa Hyde, came to Andy's defense against the faculty. "I want you to give this kid another chance. Let him go and finish the summer with the class of veterans." Concerned about integrating returning soldiers into the labor force, Congress had passed the GI Bill, which allowed veterans a stipend for college. People who had never expected to have a higher education enrolled in record numbers, and many tried for a place in the art school. Three hundred students would be attending the summer session, but the faculty promised Andy that if he did satisfactory work, he would be fully reinstated.

Luckily, Papa Hyde taught the course. After a few weeks he lectured Andy: "Damn it, you just must stop drawing in a manner that you try to please me or you're trying to get a good grade or you're trying to do someone else. You do it the way you see it. . . . You've got to do it to please yourself. And if you don't, you'll never amount to a damn."

Andy took Hyde's advice and sharpened his skills by pleasing himself. His brother Paul, back from the navy, had purchased a small truck and gave Andy a part-time job peddling fruits and vegetables door to door. When Andy wasn't helping Paul, he perched on the truck, drawing quick continuous-line sketches of the neighborhood women and children. "He used to sell the drawings for a quarter," Paul said. "He'd make a dollar or so." Over the summer, Andy's vivid impressions of women gossiping, lounging in doorways or crowding around the truck with babies slung over their hips and hanging from their skirts, filled a sketchbook.

The sketchbook got Andy back into school. He also submitted it to a competition for the school's prestigious annual award for the finest work done by a student over the summer. He won, receiving both a prize of $40 and an exhibition of his drawings. The surprised reaction was "Andy Warhola did these?" A friend from those days later said that Andy was a standout sophomore but never lost his humility and his shyness.

Andy became something of a leading figure in his class, though he was the youngest. The girls mothered him, probably misled by his slight five-foot-nine physique and pale, pale skin into thinking that he didn't have a warm coat or enough to eat. How could they know that Julia hovered, giving him the most comfortable room in the house so he would have a quiet place to work, and nagging him to bundle up? Although Oakland was only a short distance from Carnegie Tech, Andy kept his school and home lives separate.

The boys in art school also felt protective of him. Philip Pearlstein said, "Andy was a very young person. He liked to laugh. He was very naive and left himself open in a way. He was like an angel in the sky at the beginning of his college times. But only for then. That's what college gets rid of."

Andy walked the thin line between satisfying the faculty and doing things his own way. For one class the students were asked to illustrate a Willa Cather short story in which a young man leaps to his death in front of a train. The teacher expected them to do research on turn-of-the-century clothing, models of locomotives, and so on. Most of them did just that, producing accomplished renderings of a man's figure caught in the headlight of the train, or lying broken and dead on the tracks. Andy turned in a splat of red paint.

"It could be catsup," the professor said.

In his smallest voice Andy replied, "It's supposed to be blood." The teacher later argued that students should receive two grades—one for the quality of the work and one for how well it followed the assignment—but he still gave Andy an A in the class.

It was in college that Andy developed a unique drawing technique using a blotted line. To make these drawings Andy taped two pieces of paper together. On one he drew or traced an outline with his pen; then before the ink dried he quickly folded over the other piece of paper, blotting the line. It was a slow, labor-intensive procedure, but the stops, skips, and imperfections gave the line a distinctive quality. Andy's innovations attracted many followers among his fellow art students—and now when he went to the cafeteria or student "Beanery," he was surrounded by admirers.

By the third year, students had to wrestle with the prospect of earning a living, since being a full-time artist seldom paid the bills. Having grown up during the Depression, most of them, including Andy, were all too aware of the economic realities of life—and the importance of a regular paycheck. Andy considered becoming a teacher until he taught an art class at the local YMCA. Speaking in front of a group of students proved an ordeal. That left commercial art as his best career option. With that goal in mind, he concentrated his efforts on creating a portfolio of material that would appeal to the world of advertising and magazine illustration.

He also lucked into a part-time job at Joseph Horne, the top department store in Pittsburgh. For skimming through fashion magazines to get ideas for window displays, he was paid fifty cents per hour. Andy claimed he never found any ideas, but he gave a great deal of credit to his talented boss, Larry Vollmer, whom he later acknowledged as a major influence on his life. Watching Vollmer, Andy learned the real demands of commercial art, including the absolute necessity for speed.

From the window dressers, he learned other eye-opening lessons about a gay lifestyle only hinted at in college, although, according to one of his teachers, "homosexuality was pretty well accepted in art school. No one really thought much about Andy and sex because he left a very sexless impression." Young for his age, Andy was expected to go home to his mother every night after work, so his exposure to gay life was limited, but the flamboyant antics of these talented men who loved to dress up and gossip about their costume parties intrigued the innocent boy, who had yet to come out.

The summer of his junior year he and two friends took a Greyhound bus to New York to investigate the commercial art market. The drawings he pulled from a brown paper bag impressed important magazine art directors enough that they promised him freelance work after graduation. By the beginning of his senior year, Andy confidently entered a provocative painting in the juried art show given by the Pittsburgh Associated Artists. In 1948, the title alone was controversial—*The Broad Gave Me My Face but I Can Pick My Own Nose*—and the subject, a portrait of a young man with a finger buried deep in his nose, was shocking. One judge reacted in anger, declaring it vulgar and coarse. The guest judge thought it was excellent. They argued. The third judge broke the tie by casting a definitive negative vote. Retitled by Andy *Why Pick on Me,* the now notorious painting hung in a show of "rejects," where it drew a crowd of admiring students and their parents. Andy had learned the value of publicity, which he would put to good use in the future.

During his senior year, much to everyone's surprise, Andy became the only male to join the modern-dance club. He wasn't much of a dancer, but he liked the dance classes, and in photographs taken of him at the time, he often struck a dramatically angular dancer's pose. He was also a member of the film club, which sponsored avant-garde movies, and the art director of Carnegie Tech's literary magazine. He and Philip Pearlstein collaborated on a children's book about a Mexican jumping bean. The bean's name was supposed to be Leroy, but Andy misspelled it Leory, and both artists agreed it sounded better that way.

In spite of his stature in the class, Andy retained the air of the detached outsider. A friend said, "He was never argumentative, never put anybody down. He was a gentle and very kind person, and he had a whimsical smile and a wide eye, as if he was already ready to make some outlandish remark."

When Philip Pearlstein announced that he was going to New York and that one of their teachers had found him a cheap sublet on the Lower East Side, Andy's future was decided. He might not have braved New York by himself, but with Philip to lend him courage, he felt ready. In June 1949 he boarded the train with his Carnegie Tech portfolio, $200 in his pocket, and his mother's words of advice in his head: "Andy, just believe in destiny . . . you will do something great, crazy, terrific!"

Warhola to Warhol   1950–1951

I loved working when I worked at commercial art and they told you what to do and how to do it and all you had to do was correct it and they'd say yes or no. —Andy Warhol

Andy had an appointment with Carmel Snow, the elegant art director of the most elegant women's magazine in the country, *Harper's Bazaar*. He reached into the brown paper bag he carried instead of a portfolio and took out his drawings. To his dismay, a cockroach crept from between the pages onto her desk. He had introduced a live roach into this temple of high fashion. And there were plenty more at home in his apartment.

Andy loved telling stories—some truer than others—about what he later called his roach period. The bug-infested summer sublet he shared with Philip Pearlstein was in a then run-down section of New York, the Lower East Side. The grungy apartment was six flights up, bathtub in the kitchen, toilet in a closet. Living as cheaply as possible with only $200 between him and starvation, Andy urgently needed to find work. With a list of art directors in his pocket, he set out to conquer Manhattan.

New York in the 1950s was a city where men came to work in suits, white shirts, and ties. They sported felt hats in the winter and straw hats in the summer. Few women worked in offices, except as clerks or secretaries. They put on hats and gloves to come to town and wore suits or tailored dresses, pumps with high heels, and sheer flesh-toned stockings. No pantsuits or slacks were permitted on women in restaurants or offices. Everybody smoked everywhere, all the time. The three-martini lunch was a business tradition. Into this formal world entered Andy.

Philip told him, "Brush your hair! Put on a suit." Andy paid no attention. Far from trying to look like a well-dressed, worldly New Yorker, Andy cultivated a bashful, boyish air. Instead of a tailored suit, he wore chinos, T-shirts, and old sneakers. He looked like a hick from the sticks—Raggedy Andy, as his new friends teasingly called him. This was the first of the personas he assumed, or hid behind, relying on his talent to speak for him. His portfolio might harbor an occasional roach, but the drawings he pulled out impressed even the most sophisticated editor.

His first week in New York he went to see the high-powered art director Tina Fredericks at *Glamour*. The year before, she had been among those who told Andy to come back after he graduated. Fredericks said, "I greeted a pale, blotchy boy, diffident to the point of disappearance but somehow immediately and immensely appealing. His ink lines were electrifying. . . . Andy was so obviously talented I knew I wanted to use him."

She suggested he try illustrating some shoes for the

magazine. But she needed the results by the next morning. Could he do it? At ten the next day Andy returned, drawings in hand. He had rendered them in his blotted line, with a rumpled, crumpled look that suggested the shoes had been worn in some slightly funky way. Remarkable but not right, Fredericks told him. She needed to present shoes that looked new. Andy brought in revisions the following morning, and not only did Fredericks buy them, she also bought a piece of art from his portfolio and gave him another assignment. Pittsburgh was far from New York, but the lessons Andy had learned in his hometown—work hard and work fast—were already serving him well.

On his first assignment for *Glamour*—"Success Is a Job in New York"—the credit line read Warhol instead of Warhola. Andy, who liked mistakes and often incorporated them, as he had in his story of the jumping bean Leory, adopted the spelling. From now on, Warhol he would be.

His willingness to make changes endeared him to numerous art directors resigned to dealing with artists who treated advertising work with scorn no matter how much they needed the money. The fey, winsome young man with the ingratiating smile brought flowers to secretaries and willingly ran out for coffee while he waited to see their boss. He acted so helplessly naive that everyone felt sorry for him. Once he telephoned people announcing he had planted some birdseed in the park and asked if anyone wanted a bird. He knew some of his behavior was silly, but it brought in jobs, and that was what mattered to him.

At the end of the summer, when the sublet ended, Andy and Philip rented another dodgy apartment, this one an illegal space in a dance therapist's rehearsal loft. They shared a shower in the girls' dressing room and cooked on a hot plate.

After a few months the landlord evicted them. Philip was getting married, so Andy moved to a small apartment on 103rd Street, just south of Harlem. He shared this apartment with a constantly changing cast of roommates, mostly dancers, both men and women. Routinely, the women mothered Andy, cooking for him and looking after him. In return he painted a mural on one roommate's bedroom wall. (Unfortunately, her parents, who didn't know Andy would be famous, painted over it.) But when Andy talked about this time in his life, he remembered being lonely. "I kept living with roommates thinking we could become good friends and share problems, but I'd always find out that they were just interested in another person sharing the rent. At one time I lived with seventeen different people in a basement apartment on 103rd Street and not one person out of the seventeen ever shared a real problem with me."

This was the same complaint he had voiced in high school. But perhaps Andy, intent on his career, was the one guilty of not paying much attention to the people around him. Philip, who said he had no talent for the kind of commercial work Andy excelled at, commented that Andy was "a workaholic who sat at a table and worked all day and often late at night. He would do several versions of each assignment, showing all of them to art directors who loved him for that." The places where Andy lived in those early years were minimal, with few amenities or comforts. He freelanced from home, but he was capable of clearing a small space for himself and getting down to business. He hardly noticed his surroundings.

Life was not all work, however. A friend from Carnegie Tech introduced him to New York's worldly homosexual underground. While Andy didn't hide his sexual identity, even in this urbane city it was not wise to be openly gay. The police often hassled the indiscreet, and the congressional McCarthy hearings pursued not only Communists but also "homosexuals and other sex perverts." To get onto a McCarthy blacklist could destroy a career. But in spite of witch-hunters and repressive laws, New York City, with the right entrée, offered Andy varied opportunities for an active social life.

He went to many gay parties but was still too insecure to have a boyfriend. Some attributed this to his self-consciousness about his looks. Others thought he was a voyeur, more interested in watching than doing. Whatever the truth, for the time being Andy seemed content to have crushes from afar on unattainable "beauties." His biggest crush was on Truman Capote, a writer only a few years older than he, whose award-winning literary career had brought him the fame Andy wanted for himself. He took to stalking Capote, loitering outside the apartment building where the writer lived, and sending him drawings and notes, none of which Capote answered.

While never overtly aggressive, Andy possessed relentless determination in pursuit of what he wanted. Capote said, "One day my mother was visiting from Connecticut. She was sort of an alcoholic. Somehow or other my mother spoke to [Andy] out there on the street and she invited him upstairs to the apartment. I walked in later, and he was sitting there. . . . He had been having this conversation with my mother, who was a bit looped. So I sat down and talked to him."

Capote remained unimpressed, though Andy kept calling, wanting to chat. Finally Mrs. Capote answered the phone and told the crestfallen Andy to stop bothering her son. Years later, when Andy was famous, he and Capote became friends, but the writer condescendingly said of his admirer, "He seemed one of those hopeless people that you just know nothing's ever going to happen to. Just a hopeless, born loser."

Making It   1952–1959

My mother was a wonderful woman and a real good and correct artist, like the primitives. —Andy Warhol

In the spring of 1952 Julia Warhola climbed aboard her son John's ice cream truck and made the fourteen-hour drive from Pittsburgh to New York to visit "my Andy." What she found horrified her. Andy had moved out of the group apartment and was living by himself in a sordid cold-water apartment on Third Avenue under the roar of the elevated subway. He slept on a mattress, surrounded by piles of dirty laundry, heaps of reference magazines, and an army of mice. His alarmed mother, who suspected he survived on cake and candy, washed and mended his clothes, made him some home-cooked meals, then had John drive her back to Pittsburgh.

A few months later Julia returned for good. Andy might be twenty-four, but to his devoted mother it was obvious he couldn't look after himself. Since the apartment was small, Andy worked at the kitchen table, and mother and son shared the tiny bedroom, now crowded with two mattresses. Paper, pencils, brushes, and the many photographs Andy collected as source material for his illustrations littered the top of the kitchen table. He often traced elements from the photos into his drawings, transforming them in his own particular style. He worked long hours, scarcely noticing the mess around him. After finishing his assignments, he turned to his own artwork.

Shortly after Julia arrived, Andy had his first art exhibit at the Hugo Gallery—"15 Drawings Based on the Writing of Truman Capote." Andy had brought his portfolio of drawings to show to the gallery director, Alexandre Iolas. Impressed, Iolas asked the manager of the bookshop above him to keep the gallery open an extra three weeks after the last scheduled show of the season so that Andy's art could be mounted. After meeting Andy, the manager claimed that he had seldom seen anyone as plain and unprepossessing as Andy Warhol, with his broken-out face, swollen nose, bad clothes, and thinning hair. Mrs. Warhola, he added, was sweet but, in her babushka and flowered cotton housedress, looked like a cleaning lady.

Neither Truman Capote nor his mother attended the opening in June, though they did sneak in to see the whimsical drawings of boys and butterflies before the show closed. They didn't buy anything, and neither did anyone else. The press ignored the exhibit, except for one lukewarm review that compared Andy unfavorably to several other artists. Luckily, Andy's commercial art career was flourishing.

Andy courted business from art directors and editors by giving them small presents of artwork or handmade, limited-edition books that he co-wrote with various friends and then illustrated. Among the titles were *A Is an Alphabet* (1953), *25 Cats Name Sam and One Blue Pussy* (1955), and *Wild Raspberries* (1959). In 1955 he made some fantasy shoe drawings for a portfolio of prints he called A la Recherche du Shoe Perdu. Since few artists gave away their original work, Andy's gifts tended to be saved and treasured.

One such gift, a hand-painted Easter egg that Andy delivered to an art director, cemented his success as a commercial artist. The grateful editor introduced him to an agent, who quickly made Andy the most sought-after illustrator of women's accessories in New York. Proof of this came when Andy landed the plum I. Miller account. I. Miller shoes were the Manolo Blahniks of their day, a trendsetting high-end brand with a flagship Fifth Avenue store. But I. Miller's advertisements needed a new look. Andy always enjoyed drawing shoes, and his sophisticated I. Miller ads achieved iconic status for their innovative presentation and witty, offhand chic. Soon he rose to become one of the highest-paid illustrators in America, earning $50,000 a year from his I. Miller account alone, more than many presidents of corporations.

He and Julia moved from their cramped apartment under the Third Avenue el to a larger place downtown. Located at 242 Lexington Avenue, over Shirley's Pinup Bar, the new place had a spacious front room where Andy could work, and two rooms in the back. Andy continued to share a bedroom with Julia, and soon the rest of the apartment filled up with neatly stacked piles of Andy's drawings. Their menagerie of Siamese cats multiplied. About twenty kittens skittered around the apartment in wild feline games. Andy and Julia gave the cats—all named Sam—away to anyone who would take them, but they couldn't keep up with the cats' rate of reproduction. The animals ran over Andy's artwork, tore up papers, and didn't always bother to use the litter box. In spite of Julia's constant mopping and scrubbing, the apartment smelled rank. She put sheets of plastic over their mattresses during the day to protect the beds from the cats' "accidents."

By now Andy had a real boyfriend, Carl Willers. He met Carl while scouring for source photographs in the New York Public Library, where Carl worked. Years later, Andy, probably referring to Carl, said that he had his first sexual encounter when he was twenty-five and stopped when he was twenty-six. This was a typical Andy exaggeration that told more about his state of mind than the truth about his relationships. He reveled in juicy gossip about the tiniest details of other people's love affairs, but remained evasive about his own.

Yearning to be better-looking, Andy decided to take a major step and have an operation on his nose. The painful surgery reduced it slightly but did not significantly change his appearance. And Andy was losing his hair prematurely. At twenty-seven, already practically bald, he wore a cap indoors until Carl said, "Andy, this is insane. Other people think it's either phony or rude. Why don't you buy a wig?" Andy bought a wig in his natural mousy brown color, but it didn't suit his self-image at all. He then purchased the first of many wigs, ranging from gray to silver, worn with his own hair deliberately sticking out at the bottom. It became part of his signature style. Going around in his eye-catching wig, casually dressed in preppy oxford button-down shirts and paint-stained shoes, Andy might not have been a "beauty," but he would not be overlooked.

As his business grew, Andy expanded his staff. Since his college days, friends had helped him with assignments. But now he had so much work, he hired a paid studio assistant whose presence, while not exactly a secret, was not advertised to clients. He also pressed Julia into service. Andy liked the look of Julia's old-world, fanciful handwriting and had her do lettering for his commercial projects as well as the limited-edition books he made as promotion pieces. Julia even published a book of her cat drawings as "Andy Warhol's Mother." She grumbled that Andy made her work too hard, but that didn't stop her from trying to feed stuffed cabbage and dumplings to all his friends. "I am Andy Warhol," she once said—her way of showing how important she was to her son's career.

In the evenings Andy still put his friends to work, coloring in the line drawings, stretching canvases, doing whatever jobs needed to be done. Andy said it kept them from thinking too much about their problems, and he made no apologies for using their unpaid labor. Instead he took them out on the town, picking up the check at expensive restaurants and springing for orchestra seats at popular plays. Recalling those days, most of the people he commandeered said they enjoyed the work—Andy, adopting his role model Shirley Temple's attitude in movies, made everything fun. His philosophy was to keep busy, but "busy playing, because work is play when it's something you like."

Early evenings, Andy often went to Serendipity 3, an ice cream parlor on the Upper East Side. Serendipity was decorated with Tiffany lamps and an all-white mix of Victorian gingerbread, wire chairs, and marble tables. There, under the amused eyes of the three owners, he distributed sheets of black line drawings and bottles of watercolors called Dr. Martin's dyes to his friends, ordered Serendipity's gigantic ice cream sundaes, and threw coloring parties.

The owners, great admirers of Andy, took an interest in

what was happening at their back table. They offered to sell any drawings that his clients rejected. Serendipity 3 became a place where you could buy a Warhol drawing of a shoe for between $25 and $100.

Business was going well enough that when Andy's good friend Charles Lisanby, a set designer and art director at CBS, decided to make a trip around the world, Andy, who never took vacations, went along. Charles and Andy spent most weekends together sketching, but their relationship, much to Andy's disappointment, was not physical. While not attracted to Andy, Charles liked and admired him enormously. He said, "He used to be the strangest little guy, but it didn't matter. . . . Never in my life have I met anyone quite like Andy Warhol, who had that original way of seeing things to such a degree." Andy's feelings were far stronger. He hoped that traveling together would advance the relationship.

Together they journeyed across the Far East, including Japan, Indonesia, Bali, and India, before going on to Italy, France, and England. To Charles's surprise, Andy turned out to be an intrepid traveler, eager to plunge off the tourist track, willing to try the most authentic food. And though on vacation, Andy was still Andy—he never stopped drawing. Charles took home movies of Andy sketching in the midst of a group of Buddhist monks and surrounded by Balinese children who came to stare at the strange-looking American.

They were gone for six weeks, cutting a week out of the trip when Charles got food poisoning in India. Back in New York, Andy said rather bitterly that he had "gone around the world with a boy and not even received one kiss." The failure of his hoped-for romance had changed him. A friend said, "Up to that point, Andy was . . . sweet, gentle and shy and very pleasant with people . . . but when [Andy and Charles] started to break up, Andy became extremely . . . protective of himself, I feel."

Self-protective and wounded though he might be, there were still parties to give, work to do, money to make, and other young men to date. Andy's career continued to prosper. And though the critics didn't take notice, his friends praised the several small shows of his drawings. *Life* magazine did a double-page spread of his personality shoes, glittering fantasy footwear named for Zsa Zsa Gabor, Truman Capote, and other celebrities. The Museum of Modern Art even included one of his shoe drawings in a show of contemporary artists. And in 1958 the paperback book *1000 Names and Where to Drop Them* listed Andy Warhol in the "Big Business" category rather than under "Graphic Artists."

In 1960 his commercial success allowed Andy to purchase a four-story town house on Lexington Avenue. Julia moved along with him. She cooked for Andy's male friends, trying to fix them up with various female relatives back in Pittsburgh, and still nagged Andy about his clothes, about his looks, and about getting married, too. To his women friends, she sighed, "You would make a good wife for my Andy, but he is too busy." If she understood that her son was gay, she never spoke about it.

Despite his commercial achievements, Andy harbored a secret ambition. He wanted to be taken seriously as a painter. A few years earlier he had tried to join the prestigious cooperative Tanager Gallery, where his old school friend and roommate Philip Pearlstein exhibited. Philip said, "He submitted a group of boys kissing boys which the other members of the gallery hated and refused to show. He felt hurt and he didn't understand. I told him I thought the subject matter was treated too aggressively, too importantly, that it should be sort of matter-of-fact and self-explanatory. That was probably the last time we were in touch."

In other words, Andy's art was too homosexual. Other people told him the same thing. When he asked his art consultant friend Emile de Antonio (called De), whose opinion he greatly respected, why Robert Rauschenberg and Jasper Johns—two artists he both admired and knew were gay— snubbed him, De said, "Okay, Andy, if you really want to hear it straight I'll lay it out for you. You're too swish, and that upsets them. . . . these two guys wear three-button suits—they were in the navy or something." Andy admitted the answer hurt, saying, "I know plenty of painters who are more swish than me."

De agreed. "Yes, Andy, there are others who are more swish . . . but the major painters try to look straight. You play up the swish—it's like an armor with you."

In truth, in the late 1950s the New York art scene was still dominated by a group of swaggering macho geniuses, labeled Abstract Expressionists, who dripped and slashed paint across the canvas, letting their emotions rule. And New York was beginning to unseat Paris as the center for modern art. The most celebrated artist of the group, Jackson Pollock, had achieved international acclaim. Andy couldn't imagine himself in this tough, two-fisted, mostly male world where people stepped outside and threw a couple of punches to settle disputes.

Johns and Rauschenberg had given a new twist to the Abstract Expressionist mix by incorporating recognizable subjects amid their thick brushstrokes. Johns fused loosely brushed surfaces with subject matter of (mostly flat) common objects such as American flags, targets, and maps. Rauschenberg collaged images, often taken from magazines and newspapers, with found objects as widely varied as tires, a stuffed goat, and a quilt, and assembled them, calling the works that resulted combines.

De also pointed out that, unlike other artists, including Johns and Rauschenberg, Andy wasn't ashamed of being a commercial artist, and they held it against him. "They do commercial art . . . just to survive. They won't even use their real names. Whereas you've won prizes! You're famous for it."

Andy took their rejection as a quiet challenge. Only thirty-two years old, he had already reached the top both professionally and financially in a highly competitive field. He might show the world a pleasant, boyish manner, but he was not in the habit of taking no for an answer. Now he began to investigate ways to approach the next step—recognition as a serious artist.

Pop! 1960–1961

The Pop artists did images that anybody walking down Broadway could recognize in a split second. —Andy Warhol

A small drawing of a lightbulb! Ivan Karp, the savvy, fast-talking director of the Leo Castelli Gallery, was delighted to sell it to the pale young man in the gray-silver wig who had strolled in to look at artworks by Jasper Johns. Andy bargained the price down to $350.

Even though Johns and Rauschenberg still ignored Andy, he was obsessed with them, studying carefully the use of everyday objects and newspaper images in their paintings. He often dropped by the gallery just to see what they were up to. Karp, toting a cigar, his baseball cap perched on his head, looked like a character right out of a Woody Allen movie. With persuasive bravado, he prophesied that a new wave of art was on the way. To Andy, standing in this pristine town-house gallery with its white walls and curving staircase, Karp's enthusiasm was intoxicating.

Andy asked to see what else was interesting. From the stacks in the back room Karp pulled out a six-foot-tall painting of a girl in a bathing suit, holding a beach ball. It was by young artist Roy Lichtenstein, who had taken an image from a resort advertisement. The painting looked like something out of a comic book—and it startled Andy. "Oh, I'm doing work just like that," he said in a jittery voice. Curious about this strange-looking artist, Karp made a date to visit Andy's studio.

For months Andy had been working hard, trying to find a subject to paint that was both fresh and visually stimulating. He had learned from Rauschenberg, who used images from newspapers and magazines, that he did not have to start from scratch. Since he'd already been working with preexisting material in his commercial illustrations, what Rauschenberg was doing made perfect sense to him. Andy chose some black-and-white advertisements taken from the backs of cheap magazines: wigs, nose jobs, TVs, cans of food. Projecting the image in a larger format on a canvas, he traced the outlines of the ad in pencil, filling in the contours with black paint. He let the drips from his brush remain, as a nod to the freedom of the Abstract Expressionists' brushwork.

He went on to paint some of his favorite childhood comic strip characters—Popeye, Dick Tracy, Nancy (another popular cartoon). After years of pretty drawings of bows and butterflies, these images were intentionally banal and purposely ugly. He didn't try to charm or win his viewer's approval. Instead he chose small, humble, lowbrow subjects and blew them up to an important size. If new art was supposed to shock its audience, then shock them he would.

In Andy's magazine work he did as the client asked, and the result often reflected the passionate convictions of the person who hired him. He said, "I was getting paid for it and did everything they told me to do. The attitude of those who hired me had feeling; sometimes they got very emotional. The process of doing work in commercial art was machine-like, but the attitude had feeling." In Andy's own paintings, the feelings were rigorously eliminated.

Eventually he painted a six-foot-tall Coke bottle—the curvy shape reproduced straightforwardly, larger than life, with the seriousness of high art. It was a breakthrough for him. Did he intend the Coke bottle as a still life or a satire on the female figure in painting? Certainly Andy never stopped to interpret his artwork; he was just trying to reinvent himself as a serious artist.

When Karp arrived at Andy's studio, the artist met him at the door in a lopsided wig and spoke in mumbling, monosyl- labic sentences. Karp followed him down a long, dimly lit hallway past Andy's folk art collection, which included a cigar-store wooden Indian and a huge Mr. Peanut. The living room/studio, formerly a psychiatrist's office, had paneled walls and boarded-up windows. There was no sign of Andy's commercial projects, which had been hidden away for the visit. A record played the same rock song, "I Saw Linda Yesterday," over and over. Andy huddled in the shadows while Karp studied the paintings stacked against a wall. What the art dealer saw, especially the straightforward Coca-Cola bottle, excited him.

"You should do more paintings like this," he told Andy as he strode around the studio, waving his cigar.

"You can't do anything without a drip," Andy said, referring to the Abstract Expressionists' drips, by now a cliché.

"Why not?" said Karp. "Why do you have to drip?"

Andy was thrilled to hear this opinion. "That's fabulous! I don't really want to drip."

Karp believed that art in America was about to change direction and that Andy's work fit right into the new movement. Andy, so excited by Karp's visit, wrapped up a small cartoon drawing of Nancy, tied it with a ribbon, and sent it to the art dealer as a present.

Soon Karp brought some collectors to the studio. Andy greeted them wearing a feathered and sequined mask, offering his visitors masks as well. He retreated to a corner without saying a word. Karp assumed that Andy hid behind a mask to conceal his bad complexion. But it was Andy's new cool self. He told people he wanted to take all the emotion out of his work, to keep his mind blank and empty while he painted. The loud rock music, the blaring television—all were part of this effort. Letting people see that you cared one way or another while they looked at your art was "corny," according to Andy. Yet Karp, who became his friend and biggest fan, claimed that Andy was fragile, easily devastated if anyone uttered anything negative about him.

Karp convinced his boss to take a look at Andy's work, but Leo Castelli had already committed himself to showing Roy Lichtenstein, whose large cartoon paintings were done in a more precise and colorful style. There was no room in the gallery, Castelli said, for two artists using such similar subjects. And there were others using these kinds of images as well, including James Rosenquist, who painted billboard-size paintings integrating advertising and newspaper photos; Claes Oldenburg, who did soft fabric and vinyl sculpture of common objects such as telephones, ice cream cones, and hamburgers; and Robert Indiana, who made bright graphic canvases out of words. Their styles differed, but, Pop artists, as they were soon to be labeled, shared a fascination with subject matter hijacked from popular culture. Instead of surfaces thick with paint like those of the Abstract Expressionists, the texture of Pop Art paintings looked flat, with no trace of a brushtroke. Henry Geldzahler, the young assistant curator of twentieth-century painting at the Metropolitan Museum in New York said, "It was like a science fiction movie—you Pop artists in different parts of the city, unknown to each other, rising up from the muck and staggering forward with your paintings in front of you."

Both Geldzahler and Karp tried to get Andy placed in a gallery, but at the time his cartoon paintings seemed clumsy and unfinished in comparison to those by other Pop artists. So far they had been shown publicly only in the windows of a department store, as backdrops for the mannequins. In a rare outburst, Andy confronted Castelli in his office and vowed that someday he'd be back.

During this period, Andy fell into a depression. His mother constantly nagged him to send more money home to his brothers and their growing families in Pittsburgh. He felt torn between the financial security of commercial art and his ambition to be a great artist. He lay in bed, suffering from panic attacks. Afraid his heart would stop beating if he fell asleep, he would stay up all night talking on the phone to friends. It was on the telephone that he was most verbal, loving to hear gossip about celebrities and stories of his friends' love lives. Andy begged anybody and everybody for ideas. His friends grew used to hearing him moan, "What should I paint?" They made plenty of suggestions, but nothing seemed right to him.

Then one night at a party, he asked his usual question, only to receive an unusual response. Muriel Latow, an art consultant, said, "I can give you an idea, but it's gonna cost you fifty dollars." Latow had such a bright, sassy point of view that Andy believed she might well come up with a startling suggestion. He pulled out his checkbook.

"What do you like most in the world?" she asked him. "You like money. You should paint that. And you should paint something that everybody sees every day . . . like cans of soup."

Andy wrote her a check on the spot.

Soup Cans and Celebrities   1962

Pop art is for everyone. I don't think art should be only for the select few.
—Andy Warhol

The next day Andy sent Julia to the supermarket to buy every variety of Campbell's soup. Why her Andy needed all this soup she did not understand. Andy simply told her that he had loved Campbell's tomato soup as a child and remembered when it was all their family could afford for lunch. Besides, everyone recognized those striking red-and-white labels. That was why he wanted to paint them.

He did some preliminary drawings, then projected photographs of each can on a canvas and copied them in various combinations and sizes. Not long afterward, Irving Blum, a young art dealer from Los Angeles, came by to look at Andy's cartoon paintings. Blum was tall, dark-haired, and debonair, with an acquired British accent. He ambled into Warhol's studio with the confidence of someone older than his years.

To his surprise, he found Andy kneeling on the floor, hard at work on his sixteenth soup can. Lichtenstein, Andy explained, was doing cartoons too. So he had decided to paint something else. After observing the artist for several hours, Blum offered Andy his first show, at the Ferus Gallery in Los Angeles. A few months later, in July 1962, the dealer installed thirty-two individual 20" by 16" portraits of Campbell's soup cans, faithfully reproduced with their cheery red-and-white labels. He lined up the paintings on shelves, suggesting a supermarket display.

"The paintings were vividly assaulted in the press," Ivan Karp said. A gallery down the street even did a display of real Campbell's soups in their window with a sign that read, GET THE REAL THING FOR 29 CENTS. But if an ordinary meal of bread and a jug of wine could be the subject of a still life in the past, why not a soup can today? In an interview in *Time,* Andy commented, "I just paint things I always thought were beautiful, things you use every day and never think about." When asked to explain why he chose soup or money as subjects, he nonchalantly said, "I do it because I like it."

For Andy it was a triumph to be viewed in the context of the art world, rather than as a product of the advertising industry. Irving Blum had promised to sell out the show or buy the paintings himself. Whether through blind luck or sound business sense, Blum ended up buying the whole set of soup cans for $1,000, paying $100 per month till it was paid off. In 1999 he sold them to the Museum of Modern Art for $7 million in cash and a $7 million tax deduction.

What had Andy done that was so extraordinary? Other Pop artists painted found images of everyday objects but jumbled several together on one canvas. By contrast, Andy's paintings were stark, limited to one repeated image. He chose objects with a cultural punch, reproduced from the original but executed in a careless way. Lichtenstein, for example, simplified and perfected crisp cartoon images with thick, black lines and the evenly spaced red, yellow, and blue Ben Day dots of the printing process. Andy took a looser, more casual approach, permitting the accidents of smudges and dripping paint to remain, going for the effects of duplication and mass production. For small repetitions on the canvas, like columns of S&H Green Stamps, he turned to rubber and wooden stamps similar to those he used in his commercial art.

Andy continued accepting some advertising commissions to pay the rent, but at the same time he feverishly painted one canvas after another of bold, blown-up Pop images of soup cans, Coke bottles, and more. Over the summer he developed a technique that would forever change the way he worked. To paint his dollar bills faster, he decided to try silk-screening. This involves using a photographic image and transferring it onto a porous silk screen.

The process works like a stencil, using a chemically treated fabric screen in which certain areas respond to paint and others do not. To print the image, the canvas is laid out with the silk screen stretched tight over it on a wooden frame. The ink or paint is poured in a line on one inside edge of the frame, and a rubber squeegee is pulled across the mesh screen, pushing the pigment through it onto the canvas below. Using a small silk screen (approximately twelve inches square), Andy could complete this process himself in a matter of minutes and then repeat it over and over again.

The machine-made technique, so different from what the Abstract Expressionists did, furthered Andy's goal of distancing the artist from the finished product. Searching for images,

Andy again went back to his childhood for inspiration, this time to his collection of movie star photos. He began making multiple images of Elvis Presley, Warren Beatty, and Natalie Wood. One of his first silk-screened paintings was of the teenage heartthrob actor Troy Donahue, reproduced from a publicity photo in a magazine. In an ironic twist on traditional paintings, Andy used a poster meant for mass production and turned it into a painting to be viewed on its merits as an art object. And because he used the silk-screen process, he said, the images, some with too much paint or too little, could have been made by anyone. "That's probably one reason I'm using silk-screens now," he said.

The critic Rainer Crone wrote, "Warhol's paintings are potentially reproducible—they are designed to be reproduced. This casts doubt on the producer's sole authorship and strips it of its centuries old aura of uniqueness." Andy had undermined the mystique of an original, one-of-a-kind artwork with his "machine-reproduced" paintings. Yet, Andy made a policy of denying any such intellectual artistic aims. Instead he said, "I think somebody should be able to do all my paintings for me. I haven't been able to make every image clear and simple and the same as the first one. I think it would be so great if more people took up silk-screens so that no one would know whether my picture was mine or somebody else's."

Little by little Andy purposely suppressed his individuality, standing back at a distance to focus on what the subject matter suggested—whether dollar bills, movie stars, or soup cans—rather than on artistic concerns such as careful brushwork and skilled execution.

In August 1962 the actress Marilyn Monroe committed suicide, and Andy began a series of portraits of her. He made a silk screen from a publicity head shot and used it over and over in garish combinations of color. Marilyn's portrait asks the question of where the mask ends and the real Marilyn begins. People who saw Andy in his masks and later with his white-powdered face and silver wig might have wondered the same thing. Whether Andy intended to heighten the sense of tragedy in this portrait of the fallen movie queen, he never said, mumbling contradictions whenever he was pressed for explanations. But with the multiple repetitions of her image, he clearly represents Marilyn as a commodity, a product to be consumed by our materialistic culture.

The artist George Segal said, "Pop art was really an obsession with death and nihilism . . . Warhol's early images of Jackie Kennedy, Elvis Presley . . . everything was done in pastel colors, thin, bright, scintillating, but since they were about the most dense, horrifying feelings, they made a shatteringly effective statement. And Marilyn Monroe—a double obsession with style, beauty on the same extraordinary level to be admired with death and negation. A shocking juxtaposition, and I think effective."

In Andy's town house music blared, people dropped by the studio day and night, and Andy played host, offering tumblers of Scotch, eating candy, and listening in on conversations. Around this time he gave his mother, Julia, her own apartment on the street level of the town house, joking that he'd sent her to live in the basement. He claimed that the upstairs was getting too crowded. Perhaps, still keeping his own dating life a secret from the family, he worried that Julia would see something upsetting. Certainly he tried to protect his mother from his friends, even warning them not to swear around her. So aside from forays to shop or clean the house, Julia stayed downstairs for the next twelve years, surrounded by her ever-growing piles of shopping bags and papers, Siamese cats, and a large parrot.

Andy's brothers objected to their mother's banishment, claiming that Bubba, as she was called by her grandchildren, was lonely. Paul or John, along with their wives and children, drove in every few months, landing on Andy's doorstep for a surprise visit. Andy seemed glad to see them and put the children to work stretching canvases, but he didn't introduce them to his friends or take them out to parties. As he had done at college, he kept his family and friends in separate compartments. With the grandchildren around to keep her company, Bubba cooked and talked nonstop.

Andy's reputation for eccentricity included his unconventional living arrangements with his mother. He added to his myth by telling stories about Julia, saying she lived in the basement and drank a case of whiskey every week. In reality, ground-floor apartments were commonplace in the city, and Andy gave Julia plenty of spending money, most of which she used to send care packages home to her family or stuffed carelessly in a fat glass jar. When he offered to buy her a house on Long Island, she refused to go. She would stay near her Andy.

Meanwhile Andy led a busy social life, showing up at openings and parties, pushing himself to be seen, singing in a rock band with friends (although he couldn't sing), and trying desperately to find a reputable gallery to represent him in New York. Even without the support of a dealer willing to give him a show, he continued working, creating hand-painted canvases as well as silk screens of single and multiple images. With typical irreverence, he chose as his subjects copies of paint-by-number kits of sailboats and flowers, diagrams of dance steps, enlarged matchbook covers, portraits of 1930s movie stars and English royalty, and more soup cans and Coke bottles.

Splotches of paint stayed put. Unintended cropping of a picture remained. Yet the process itself, with all its accidents and variations, was innovative. Somehow, within the framework of mass production, there was a sense of artistry in Andy's series of Coke bottles and Marilyn paintings. And while he used assistants, Andy made the decisions. He might ask for ideas, but he followed his own instincts with an uncanny ability to choose subjects that eventually captured and held the public's imagination. For Andy, the early sixties proved to be a period of volcanic creativity. During those years, he produced a staggering amount of groundbreaking work.

The curator Henry Geldzahler had become "a five-hours-a-day-on-the-phone/see-you-for-lunch/quick-turn-on-the-*Tonight Show* friend." At one of these lunches Geldzahler showed Andy a newspaper with the headline "129 Die in Jet Crash." What about more serious subject matter? he asked. Andy felt that Pop came from the outside, so getting an idea from someone else was no different from finding one in a magazine. And always, he had a gift for recognizing a good idea when he heard one. He already had hand-painted several other newspaper front pages, so now he made a painting titled *129 Die in Jet (Plane Crash)*. Although crudely executed, it foreshadowed themes of death and destruction that he would tackle later. Dissatisfied for the moment with the result, though, Andy went back to painting soup cans and portraits.

He still obsessed that without a major gallery, the Pop Art parade would pass him by. "No matter how good you are, if you're not promoted right, you won't be remembered," he said. Finally his friend De introduced him to an important dealer named Eleanor Ward. An art world figure known for her flair, Ward owned the prestigious Stable Gallery (located in a former stable). As she told it, she had the month of November open but no artist to show. And then, as she relaxed in her country house, she clearly heard a voice. "I was lying there on my back, sunning, with my eyes closed, not thinking about anything in the world, and suddenly a voice said 'Andy Warhol.' . . . So I immediately went into the house, looked up Andy's number, called—this is the first time in my life that I'd ever called him. He answered the telephone and I told him who I was. And I said, 'Can I come and look at your work?' And he said, 'Wow!' And so we made an appointment." She later claimed that the mysterious voice must have been her guardian angel.

Forceful and intimidating in her designer suit and stiletto heels, Eleanor Ward marched into Andy's studio, peered quickly at the work, then sat around for a few hours, chatting and drinking whiskey out of white Danish cups, with De and the nervous artist. De finally pushed her to make a decision. Ward pulled out her wallet and said, "Well, I'll give you a show, but you've got to paint a two-dollar bill for me." Most artists would have told her off. "Wow!" was all Andy said.

Soon Eleanor Ward's lucky two-dollar bill was immortalized in paint, and she gave Andy his first important show in New York. It was the height of the fall art season—November 1962. Along with the two-dollar-bill paintings hung multiple portraits of Elvis Presley, Marilyn Monroe, and the now notorious soup cans. New Yorkers couldn't decide whether Andy was serious or perpetrating a gigantic joke at their expense, but they flocked to see his startling artwork.

A story circulating at the time reflected the public's ambivalence. Two directors of the Museum of Modern Art met in the street. One asked, "Have you seen the Andy Warhol show?"

"Isn't it awful?" asked the second.

"Yes," said the first, "I bought one."

Indeed, the show sold out, including *Gold Marilyn Monroe,* purchased for $800 by the great modern architect and arbiter of taste Philip Johnson. Andy's old pals, as well as a host of artists and journalists, milled about, and Eleanor Ward passed out soup can buttons, while the artist stood alone in a corner. Finally, after ten years in New York, Andy Warhol had achieved his dream of fame, but would his soup cans prove to be a hoax or the real thing?

51

Fame! 1963

In the future everybody will be world famous for fifteen minutes.
—Andy Warhol

In a sport jacket and tie, Andy slouched, hands folded, on a stage in front of one of his Elvis Presley paintings. A camera rolled.

"I really don't know what to say," said Andy to his interviewer. "Just put the words in my mouth and I'll say them."

"Why did you and Lichtenstein and other Pop artists use cartoons?" asked the interviewer.

"We just read a lot of comic books," replied Andy. "Comic books tell us a lot. Living in New York is like being in a Western movie."

Andy refused to defend himself against skeptics who declared that Pop Art was all an elaborate joke. He preferred to go on painting what he pleased despite his critics. When someone commented that anybody could do what he did without much effort, he agreed. Was he romanticizing the crassness of American life? Or was he satirizing it? Did he really think soup cans were an appropriate subject for art?

Critics wanted him to make his intentions clear. But he never did, preferring to dodge direct questions, stand by without comment, or say something off-the-wall. Andy was not the only artist who avoided discussing his intentions. Like others, he believed it was up to the artist to make art and up to the viewer to discover its meaning. What was distinctive about Andy was his responses.

The media decreed Andy a sensation and a celebrity, but how would he hold on to his newfound status? He need not have worried. By 1963 many major museums were mounting an exhibit of Pop Art—a name that had captured the art world's imagination—and from New York to California, all the group shows included a painting by Andy Warhol. Mass audiences, who had been bewildered by Abstract Expressionism, found themselves attracted to these realistic new works. They might not have understood the canvases of Jackson Pollock with their drips and splatters and interlacing lines, but they recognized and related to an image of Marilyn Monroe or Coke bottles. A new generation of artists, collectors, galleries, and critics would embrace Pop Art.

Andy's brash paintings evoked a multitude of responses. The artist's attitude was simple: Whether the public loved it or hated it, he was going to make more and more art. In an interview in *Time,* he said, "The things I want to show are mechanical. Machines have less problems. I want to be a machine, wouldn't you?"

Now the other artists at Leo Castelli's, including Johns and Rauschenberg, finally accepted Andy as one of the gang, a worthy colleague and competitor. So far, with the exception of a painting of Rauschenberg, all of Andy's silk-screened portraits had been of celebrities he had never met. His first commissioned portrait for a client was of Ethel Scull, the wife of a New York mogul, who owned a fleet of yellow cabs called Scull's Angels.

"In a way," said De, "he's [Robert Scull] the oddest figure out of this whole scene, because at one level he's coarse beyond description—beyond imagination! And yet at another, he really saw what was going on and put his money out." Husband and wife, both passionate collectors of contemporary art, already owned several Warhol paintings.

Ethel, fresh from the hairdresser and wearing a stylish Yves St. Laurent suit, picked Andy up in a taxi and, to her astonishment, was taken to a penny arcade in Times Square. Andy ushered her into a photo booth, where a strip of four instant photos could be taken for twenty-five cents. He dropped a roll of quarters into the slot and ordered her to pose. They ran from one booth to the next, Andy prodding Ethel to smile, laugh, vamp, and pout. One hundred shots later Andy and Ethel emerged into the sunlit street, clutching handfuls of small black-and-white photographs.

Andy chose seventeen poses, mixed and matched them, repeated a few, and presented the Sculls with a multiple-image portrait of Ethel, thirty-six black-and-white photos on colored backgrounds, processed into 20" by 16" silk screens. He captured Ethel in many different moods, revealing aspects of her personality that she herself had not realized. When Scull asked Andy in what order to put them together, Andy replied that the order didn't matter. Scull should assemble them any way he liked.

Making a portrait with multiple images, multiple points of view, was a method particular to Warhol, never used before by another artist, and now widely copied. The single-frame images remind us of movie stills, suggesting a cinematic progression. By using the silk-screen technique, the artist could work from photographs, rather than live models, and choose subjects ranging from Ethel Scull to politicians and movie stars, mug shots of criminals, or even a reproduction of the famous *Mona Lisa* by Leonardo da Vinci.

To accommodate all his canvases, as well as visitors dropping by, Andy rented an old firehouse from the city to use as a work space; his studio/living room was too cramped. In one month he'd painted a hundred pictures, and the paint covered every surface. The new space had no heat or electricity, so Andy didn't have the distraction of phone calls. Unfortunately the roof leaked, so each night he rolled up his completed canvases and carried them home. In his usual frenzy, he managed to make dozens of new works.

Andy's canvases were getting bigger, and the physical labor involved in making the silk screens was more than he could handle. To help out at the firehouse he hired Gerard Malanga, a handsome twenty-one-year-old poet who, like Andy, came from a poor family and was eager to make a name for himself in New York. Gerard also knew how to silkscreen, as he had been a summer intern for a textile manufacturer. His job was to help Andy pull the squeegee across the screen and also to wipe out excess ink before it dried and clogged the holes. The first project was a series of 40" by 40" paintings of Elizabeth Taylor. Gerard described the process: "The image . . . a . . . face, . . . lips, . . . eye shadow, painted in by hand with liquitex over a hand-painted background. The silkscreen is applied, laid down over the abstract color shapes . . . black silkscreen paint [is] squeegeed across the entire screen in one motion."

Gerard felt a little frightened of the silent, chalk-faced artist. Andy looked like an alien to him; Gerard wondered about his motives. Only after Andy took him home to meet his mother, who served them 7-Up and hamburgers on white bread, did Gerard begin to relax. He glanced around the living room and recognized the paintings of Campbell's soup cans he had been reading about in art magazines. Finally he realized who his employer was.

The two men had a lot in common. Both loved parties, movie posters, and famous film stars, and soon they were stepping out on the town every night, going to parties, poetry readings, and experimental dance performances, referring to each other as Gerry Pie and Andy Pie.

Gerard said, "If you were to meet him for the first time, and Andy liked you, he became your instant fan, and this in turn, would create in you a feeling of self-esteem. It's as if he were collecting people. He has a hypnotic power to create a personality for someone . . . the secret of Andy's success was his own self-effacement."

With Gerard's help, Andy returned to the subject of death he'd briefly explored in *129 Die in Jet (Plane Crash)*. The paintings, titled the Disaster Series, were taken from magazines and tabloid newspaper photographs. Many of these images depicted morbid scenes—an auto accident with a bleeding body half out of a crumpled car, a suicide leap from the Empire State Building, or policemen with clubs and dogs charging unarmed citizens. The energy and enthusiasm that his new friend and assistant brought to the studio spurred Andy on. "Each painting took about four minutes, and we worked as mechanically as we could, trying to get each image right," said Gerard, "but we never got it right. By becoming machines we made the most imperfect works. As always, Andy embraced the mistakes. . . . 'It's just part of the art.' "

All of Andy's paintings, especially the portraits, have a cold, austere quality, but nowhere is his distanced style more apparent than in the Disaster Series. Perhaps he could push back his fear of and obsession with death, control it, by reproducing one violent image after another. "I realized everything I was doing must be death," Andy said. "It was Labor Day and every time you turned on the radio, they said something like, 'Four million are going to die.' That started it. But when you see a gruesome picture over and over again, it doesn't have any effect."

America itself was a hotbed of unrest. The military was building up its presence in Vietnam. Demonstrators marched on Washington for civil rights. Martin Luther King Jr. gave his famous "I Have a Dream" speech. Andy could not help being influenced by the changing world around him. Yet he insisted that "there was no profound reason for doing a death series . . . there was no reason for doing it at all, just a surface reason."

When asked if Andy was interested in political questions, Henry Geldzahler, who continued to follow Andy's career, said, "He would never never never never say that it has a meaning but it does. For instance in . . . *Race Riot* he is clearly not on the side of the dogs or the policemen. But if you ask him he would say 'oh um, um, um, hm.' But [what is] important is what is left on the canvases—the result." Andy's *Race Riot* silk screens are based on a photograph that appeared in the May 1963 issue of *Life*. The photo showed a clash between civil rights demonstrators and police in Birmingham, Alabama.

De agreed. "Andy pretends he has no politics. I think it's

very hard to be the son of Czech immigrants, when your father was a manual worker, living in Pittsburgh, and not to develop political ideas." In the same way that television bombards the viewer with live repetitions of disasters in a kind of you-are-there realism, until repetition numbs the horror, Warhol's cold, repetitive canvases play with our perceptions. The viewer is drawn in by pattern and intense hues, despite the grisly details. The colorful squares, in such paintings as *Green Burning Car 1,* achieve a graphic effect. The Disaster Series paintings become powerful images because of the apparent contradiction between the tragic subject and the mechanical style. With his usual irony, Andy said, "The more you look at the exact same thing, the more meaning goes away and the better you feel."

He chose another loaded subject, the electric chair, one of America's most controversial methods of capital punishment. Whether the viewer finds these paintings hypnotic or monotonous, the effect of the grim hot seat in paintings such as *Electric Chair* is disconcerting. When Andy mounted his first gallery show in Paris the next year, one review announced, "The [Disaster] pictures become holy scenes in a godless world." The French loved them. This marked the beginning of Andy's huge following in Europe. Yet American collectors did not want to hang such disturbing pictures on their walls, in spite of Andy's bon mot "You'd be surprised who'll hang an electric chair in the living room. Especially if the background matches the drapes." Even his brothers wouldn't take one. As for his friends, they remained unimpressed. Eleanor Ward refused to show them. If Andy was just painting to make money, as he was often accused of doing, why did he concentrate on such tough subjects?

According to Henry Geldzahler, what turned Andy on was

precisely such loaded, supercharged images. "What held his work together in all media was the absolute control Andy had over his own sensibility, a sensibility as sweet and tough, as childish and commercial, as innocent and chic as anything in our culture."

Today the Disaster Series is considered to be among his greatest, most riveting works. Still Andy insisted, "I'm not a social critic. I just paint those objects in my paintings because those are the things I know best. I'm not trying to criticize the US in any way, not trying to show up any ugliness at all: I'm just a pure artist."

Having left his commercial career behind, Andy might have thought of himself as a pure artist, but the life he led was far from pure. It was not only Andy the cutting-edge artist but also Andy the celebrity with the cutting-edge lifestyle that both shocked and fascinated the public. The drug culture, gay liberation, and the sexual revolution would hit America in the mid-sixties like a tidal wave picking up momentum as it rolled from New York to California. At the crest of it was Andy, spouting remarks such as "I don't believe in love" and "I want to be a machine."

Made in America   1963–1964

I like boring things. I like things to be the same over and over again.
—Andy Warhol

Andy and his boyfriend, a young stockbroker turned poet named John Giorno, sat in the Film-Makers' Cooperative theater watching a midnight screening of an underground horror movie. "How terrible," Andy muttered in the dark to John. "Movies should be beautiful. I could do better than these." Although he had no idea how to shoot a movie, or even load or focus a camera, Andy bought a Bolex 8mm camera.

One night John woke up and found Andy staring at him.

"What are you doing?" John asked.

"Watching you sleep," came the reply.

Andy loved to watch people. His idea of making a movie consisted of turning on a camera and letting it run. As wowed as Andy was by Hollywood movies, experimental or underground films offered him more in terms of making his own statement. He told John he could be a movie star.

"What do I have to do?" asked John.

"I want to make a movie of you sleeping," replied Andy. That was fine with John, as he spent most of his leisure time sleeping anyway. For two weeks, Andy turned the camera on automatic, focusing on the sleeping Giorno, nude but modestly draped, for four hours at a stretch. But when he took the film in to be developed, Andy found out that he'd forgotten to rewind the camera properly, ruining all the film. He had to reshoot the entire movie.

While the new rolls were being processed, Andy, the self-invented new moviemaker, went off to Hollywood. Irving Blum at the Ferus Gallery was exhibiting Andy's Elvis Presley paintings. The life-size portraits, silk-screened in black on a silver background, featured Elvis with his six-gun pointed at the viewer. Taken from a publicity still of the rock-and-roll king playing the role of a cowboy, the paintings seemed perfect for Los Angeles, home of Hollywood and movie mania. The most arresting canvases showed multiple images of Elvis flickering across the canvas like frames from a reel of film.

Andy shipped a canvas roll of silver Elvises and a package of wooden stretchers to Blum with casual instructions to cut the canvas up and stretch it any way he wanted. When Blum called to check, Andy reassured him. Just make sure to hang them, sides touching, across the four walls of the gallery, he told the dealer. Dumbfounded that the artist could leave such decisions up to him, Blum laid the canvas roll on the floor and proceeded to cut it apart. Then he hung the Elvises as Andy had directed.

Meanwhile Andy and three friends, Gerard Malanga, an actor named Taylor Mead, and Win Chamberlain, an artist, drove three thousand miles to L.A. Andy planned the road trip because Julia had made him paranoid about flying. "Many a big shot guy in the sky might die," she announced. Since he had never learned to drive, Andy spent most of the trip lounging on a mattress in the back of a beat-up Ford station wagon. With Top 40 pop songs such as "Puff the Magic Dragon" and "If I Had a Hammer" blasting on the radio, the group of oddball young men barreled across America, pausing at truck stops and diners along the way. Andy reveled in the attention they attracted. Even though no one had ever heard of Andy Warhol in Kansas or Arizona, people knew by looking at him that they were in the presence of an exotic bird.

While America stared at Andy, he stared back at America. The artist had flown around the world but had never been west of Pittsburgh, and the view out of the car window thrilled him. "The farther west we drove to California, the more Pop everything looked on the highways," he said, referring to the roadside architecture and billboard advertisements. "Suddenly we all felt like insiders because even though Pop was everywhere, most people still took it for granted; whereas we were dazzled by it. To us, it was the new art. Once you 'got' Pop you could never see a sign the same way again. And once you thought Pop, you could never see America the same way again."

The actor Dennis Hopper (now best known for the cult film *Easy Rider*) gave Andy a gala party in Hollywood with the younger generation of movie actors, including Troy Donahue, whose portrait Andy had painted the year before. Andy also attended an opening for Pop artist Claes Oldenburg and another party at the Pasadena Museum for celebrated European artist Marcel Duchamp. Duchamp said of Andy's art, "If you take a Campbell's Soup can and repeat it fifty times, you are not interested in the retinal image. What interests you is the concept that wants to put fifty Campbell's Soup cans on a canvas." Critics thought the image of the soup can was radical. Duchamp understood that what was radical was the *idea* of painting a soup can.

Despite the throng that crowded into the Ferus Gallery, not one of the huge paintings, even modestly priced at $1,000, sold, and the reviews of the show were dismal. "Warhol doesn't suggest in any of his works that he is an artist," one critic wrote. Posterity disagrees. Today most of Andy's Elvis portraits are owned by major museums. Art critic Ingrid Sischy explained: "Even when the Pop Art explosion happened . . . there was still the sense that it was fluff. Sure there were critics, dealers, and collectors who recognized his genius . . . but there was also a lot of eyebrow raising and much dismissing."

During his stay in California Andy shot another movie, entitled *Tarzan and Jane Regained . . . Sort of,* starring Taylor Mead. He used a handheld camera and shot most of it in his bathroom at the Beverly Hills Hotel. Claes Oldenburg and Dennis Hopper played bit parts.

Managing the growing entourage of young people who flocked around him, eager to go to parties and be in his films, proved difficult for Andy. He alternated between passivity and temper tantrums. Though he and Gerard Malanga didn't have a physical relationship, he flew into a jealous rage when Gerard, assuming that Andy would be out late, brought a girl back to their shared hotel room. The aloof, ironic Andy that emerged in interviews and at art events was a conscious pose he constructed. It was his way of staying in control, protecting himself. Later Andy would write,

"So what." That's one of my favorite things to say.
"My mother didn't love me."
So what.
"I'm a success but I'm still alone."
So what.
I don't know how I made it through all the years
before I learned how to do that trick.

Andy punished Gerard for his L.A. fling by refusing to give him taxi fare to get home after they drove back to New York. Gerard said that although his boss usually was generous about expenses, this time he had to drag his heavy suitcase onto the subway. The next day, however, they were both back at work, silk-screening the Disaster Series at the firehouse and making more films.

Andy's choices of subjects in his art, from celebrities to disaster headlines, may not have been considered worthy by intellectual critics, but Andy used his instincts as a barometer, zeroing in on the pulse of the times. On November 22, 1963, in Dallas, President John Kennedy was assassinated. The whole country sat glued in front of their televisions as the coverage ran nonstop images of the president being shot and his wife, Jackie, trying to shield her wounded husband. Andy responded by silk-screening portraits of Jackie Kennedy, one of the most popular First Ladies in the history of the United States. The portraits are based on four head shots taken of Jackie immediately before and after the shooting and at the funeral. *16 Jackies,* the sixteen-panel multiple-image portrait in blues and grays, is both moving and deeply respectful of his subject. Consistent with his use of preexisting images, newspaper photographs were the source of the silk screens. This is classic Warhol—distancing, yet gripping. He made separate canvases for each image, hanging them side by side, instead of repeating the image on a single canvas. Like the rows upon rows of icons he had seen in church as a boy, the portrait of Jackie achieved an emblematic effect. Over the years he would go back and forth between these two methods of replicating images in his artwork.

At the beginning of 1964 Andy vacated the firehouse studio and moved to a warehouse space on the fifth floor of a loft building not far from Grand Central Station. The warehouse boasted a view of the Empire State Building, a freight elevator, and a telephone booth. Here Andy had room to paint, make movies, entertain guests, and house his growing band of friends, assistants, and hangers-on. Because of the tremendous amount of film and painting turned out there, the space became known as the Factory. Calling it a studio sounded too elitist to an artist who wanted to be a machine. A studio, after all, implied a private place, where artists worked in isolation. At the Factory, the name itself associated with mass production, many activities went on at the same time, including the collaborations that fired his art. As the lines between his work life and his social life blurred, Andy Warhol's Factory soon would be notorious.

The Swinging Silver Factory   1964

A lot of people thought it was me everyone at the Factory was hanging around. . . . I just paid the rent and the crowds came around simply because the door was open. . . . They came to see who came. —Andy Warhol

A lighting designer for off-Broadway shows, Billy Linich (who later rechristened himself Billy Name), invited Andy over to see his apartment on the Lower East Side. There Billy lived with several creative young men, all openly gay. Andy found them interesting, especially their lack of pretense about their sexual orientation. Billy, on an amphetamine high, had painted his apartment silver and covered it in tinfoil. "Silver was the future, it was spacey—the astronauts . . . And silver was also the past—the Silver Screen," wrote Andy. He commissioned Billy to design the new Factory. Using gallons of paint, Billy turned a brick wall into a sheet of gleaming silver, then proceeded to spray the tables, the chairs, the pay phone, even the toilet. The walls, pipes, and ceiling arches were papered with so much aluminum foil that the whole place took on the look of a futuristic fantasy. Even the floor had a coat of silver paint, which had to be redone every two weeks because of the constant flow of people tramping in and out.

The result, photographed many times, fired the public's imagination and added to the Factory's reputation as a hot spot and the center for the Pop Art in-crowd. Henry Geldzahler said, "It became a sort of glamorous clubhouse with everyone trying to attract Andy's attention." Billy's own imagination was so stimulated that he moved into a bathroom and slept on the floor so that he could work day and night. Every week or two he asked Andy for twenty dollars for food.

A tall string bean who moved in a slow rhythm, good-natured Billy wanted only to be part of it all. In addition to his other skills, he also was a talented street scavenger of furniture and leftover items New Yorkers placed on the curb for trash pickup. One day he found an abandoned maroon couch on the street and dragged it upstairs. Andy used it as a prop for his film *Couch,* in which people engaged in various activities, from talk to sex, on its worn cushions.

Billy, who had learned barbering in his grandfather's shop, gave the staff haircuts. It inspired Andy to do a twenty-three-minute film of Billy cutting someone's hair, an exercise in tedium for the baffled viewer. But tedium, stories with no beginning, middle, or end, elementary camera techniques, minimal editing, a stationary camera, and duplication comprised the main elements of Andy's film oeuvre. Often he didn't arrange the reels in sequence. This spatial, non-narrative approach to filmmaking had a correspondence in abstract art as well as in the experimental poetry and fiction of the 1960s. Certainly there is a correlation in terms of the serial imagery in Andy's artworks, the haphazard arrangement of repeated images, the accidents of blotched paint or "mistakes" left in, unedited. The films were a natural extension of his painting.

One of Warhol's best-known films of that period is called *Eat* (1964), starring Robert Indiana, the Pop artist whose paintings featuring the word *LOVE,* stenciled in bright combinations of colors, commented on the sixties peace/love movement. Andy instructed Indiana to slowly eat one mushroom while the camera ran for thirty minutes.

Seated on a high-backed carved wooden chair, wearing a hat and a sweater, the artist impassively nibbled away, looking from the camera to the sun shining down from the studio window. The only relief from the monotony is Indiana's cat, who hops onto his shoulder and is offered a bite. In the last reel Indiana sits happily picking his teeth, no mushroom in sight. Because the reels are not in order, the mushroom appears, disappears, and reappears, adding to the viewer's confusion.

Confusion was just what Andy was after. If art imitates life, weren't confusion and monotony right on the mark? Life goes on and on without interruption, and so did his films. They provoked a great deal of discussion. In fact, one New York critic reported spotting more people in the lobby talking about *Eat* than in the theater watching it. In Los Angeles most of the audience demanded their money back.

No matter what people said about the quality and content, Andy made more films in six months than most filmmakers do in a lifetime. In December 1964 he won the Sixth Annual Film Culture Award. Instead of attending the ceremony, Andy sent a film of himself staring vapidly into space, passing the award, a basket of produce, back and forth to some friends who slowly ate the contents.

Most people expressed bafflement, arguing that Andy didn't deserve the award and citing the usual complaint that Warhol films were tedious and repetitive. Jonas Mekas, a leading figure in independent films and the founder of the journal *Film Culture,* disagreed: "The work was to us very impressive. . . . He stopped everything dead, like beginning from scratch and forcing us to reevaluate, to see, to look at everything from the beginning. . . . here is somebody who is doing original work that inspired us." Andy didn't defend himself against his critics, but he did point out that television was mind-numbing, too, with "the same plots and the same shots over and over again."

"Apparently," Andy said, "most people like watching the same basic thing as long as the details are different. But I'm just the opposite. If I'm going to sit and watch the same thing I saw the night before, I want it to be exactly the same."

Despite Andy's blasé explanations, his techniques were not as simple as they seemed. He was always experimenting. One new technique involved flicking the camera on and off while he filmed a scene. This "strobe cut" interrupted the action with a blank film frame that played as a flash of white. It further removed the audience from the story, reminding the viewer that it was just a movie after all. But estrangement from society lay at the heart of Andy's films, not only in his characters, who purge themselves for the camera, but also through his handling (or mishandling, some might say) of the technical process. "If you want to know all about Andy Warhol, just look at the surface of my paintings and my films, and there I am. There's nothing behind it."

While Andy's remarks couldn't always be taken at face

value, they often held a deeper truth. The surface of his paintings reveals much about his style—flat, thick lines, gaudy color, a machine-induced image. And on another level, the word *surface* might refer to the surface preoccupations of our culture—a world of appearances that Andy saw around him every day and night at the Factory.

In April 1964 the architect Philip Johnson, who had become an advocate of Andy's work since purchasing *Gold Marilyn Monroe,* commissioned him to do a mural for the New York State Pavilion at the World's Fair in New York. As might have been expected, what Andy delivered caused a furor. He installed a 20' by 20' black-and-white mural called *The Thirteen Most Wanted Men,* consisting of mug shots of alleged Mafia suspects taken from an out-of-date FBI list at the New York Police Department. Governor Nelson Rockefeller said it insulted his Italian constituents. Philip Johnson told Andy he had twenty-four hours to remove the mural. "Well," said Andy, "let's replace it with pictures of the head of the fair." Johnson was furious. So was Andy, who had the mural covered with silver paint.

Later that month Andy caused another uproar with his new exhibit at the Stable Gallery by filling the space with rows of hand-painted and silk-screened cardboard Brillo boxes. Andy had made them at the Factory in a production line with assistants over a period of six weeks. "I want it to look like a warehouse," he said. Crowds who waited in lines around the block to see the exhibit barely squeezed into the narrow aisles stacked with artwork. Later, at a party given by Robert and Ethel Scull at the Factory, Andy's celebrity portraits were displayed on the silver walls and Brillo boxes were stacked up on the floor. It was the first time those outside the inner circle were invited in.

Andy imagined people walking out of the Stable Gallery with purchased boxes under their arms. It didn't happen. Critic and curator Arthur Danto outspokenly said that Warhol's Brillo Boxes of 1964 brought the history of Western art to a close. Despite the press and the hoopla, people didn't know what to think about the boxes, and almost nothing sold. The Sculls, irritated by the circus atmosphere at their party and the fact that the press ignored them, canceled their Brillo Box purchase.

Disappointed and worried about paying his ever-growing bills, Andy decided to end his relationship with Eleanor Ward and the Stable Gallery. It was time to join Leo Castelli, who by now was delighted to represent Andy Warhol, the most talked-about artist of the decade. With a major gallery behind him, Andy hoped to be not only a media success but a financial one as well. Andy Warhol had joined the big boys of the Pop Art movement.

The Prince of Pop 1964

Don't think about making art, just get it done. Let everyone else decide whether it's good or bad, whether they love it or hate it. While they're deciding, make even more art. —Andy Warhol

During the heady days and nights of the mid-sixties, Andy and his group traveled in a pack to parties and rock concerts, drawing attention wherever they appeared. Andy had changed his look from casual preppie in bow tie and paint-stained shoes to tough guy in "a muscle man's S&M black leather jacket, tight black jeans [under which he wore panty hose], T-shirts, high-heeled boots, dark glasses and a silver wig to match his silver Factory." Surrounded by a changing band of good-looking boys and girls, Andy rarely spoke in public except to say something terse and witty. In a flat, expressionless voice, he repeated "Wow" or "Marvelous" or "I don't know" to people barraging him with questions. And wherever he went, he carried a tape recorder, his "wife, Sony" to eavesdrop and record conversations that were transcribed by eager assistants the next day.

Some thought he was arrogant, but his aloofness was a conscious pose. Close friends said he was chatty and curious, always ready to listen to their confidences. He was their leader, accepting and encouraging their excesses. They, in turn, loved and felt strangely protective of him. "The Factory," Andy said, "was a place where you could let your problems show, and nobody would hate you for it. And if you worked your problems up into entertaining routines, people would like you even more for being strong enough to say you were different and actually have fun with it."

The "entertaining routines" were fueled by the beginning of what has been called the swinging drug culture. The Factory attracted the wild, clever party set. Now, instead of entertaining at his town house, Andy centered his social life on the Factory. With the eyes of a voyeur, Andy, who took prescription diet pills but did not use harder recreational drugs, watched while his entourage literally and figuratively lived the high life. Drag queens from Queens mingled with social butterflies from the Upper East Side. Harvard graduate students partied with leather-clad muscle boys. Lowlifes and the elite of New York came together.

Among the cast of characters were Gerard Malanga, who continued to work as Andy's assistant, and Billy Name, who acted as photographer and ringmaster of Andy's complicated life. The wildest of all were Billy's friends, who wandered in and out of the Factory at all hours. Called the amphetamine rapture group or the mole people, many of them aspired to act, dance, or create their own art, but, agitated by speed, they expressed themselves in extreme behavior. Ondine, who appeared in many of Andy's movies, mesmerized everyone with his intensity and verbal acrobatics. As for Rotten Rita, Silver George, and Stanley the Turtle, their names alone defied conventional middle-class decorum.

Andy discovered his share of outrageous personalities, among them the French beauty Comtesse Isabelle Dufresne. He told her she should change her name, suggesting Poly Ester or Notre Dame. Isabelle came up with Ultra Violet. "It will be an ear-catcher," pronounced Andy. To give her a new look to go with her new name, Andy took her on a shopping spree at a secondhand store. There she tried on a vintage violet velvet dress, slightly torn at the hem. "That's the torn look," said Andy, and Ultra Violet bought it. In return for putting her in his movies, the French aristocrat took Andy to parties with the international set.

One of Billy's friends, Brigid Berlin (aka the Duchess or Brigid Polk), the debutante daughter of a rich Fifth Avenue family, was one of Andy's most loyal followers. Her problems included binge eating and a big amphetamine habit. As an overweight eleven-year-old, she had been prescribed diet pills and become hooked on speed. Her uninhibited behavior and gift of gab amused Andy, who defended her even when she ranted and raved against him. Andy always loved talkers even more than he loved "beauties." For twenty years he and Brigid usually telephoned each other once a day, chatting for hours. Brigid also accompanied him to the gym three times a week, where she said Andy tried to build up his pectorals. She became Andy's muse for Polaroid photographs and for his tape-recorded conversations.

Another socialite, Baby Jane Holzer, promptly rose to be one of the early Warhol Superstars. This was a label Andy adopted from Ingrid Superstar to anoint actors in his films. A "beauty" with a leonine mane of blond hair, designer clothes, and social connections, she also was designated the first Girl of the Year. Wherever Andy and Baby Jane went together the media snapped their picture. Andy loved seeing himself in the society/gossip columns. Photogenic women on his arm meant more picture opportunities. He also enjoyed filming the homes of the well-heeled people Baby Jane knew, bringing along his whole entourage. Unfortunately, they often pocketed whatever small objects with resale value caught their eyes.

Anyone can be a film star, Andy said to lure interesting people or "beauties" to the Factory for a Screen Test—three to four minutes of tightly framed close-ups of their faces. Shot at twenty-four frames a second, and projected at a lower speed of sixteen frames per second, the head shots had a spacey, dreamy quality. Those who auditioned stood in front of a stationary camera. Andy rolled the film, told the subject not to move, not even blink, and then walked away. Not everybody paid attention to his directions. Baby Jane unwrapped and licked a piece of gum. In another screen test, she brushed her teeth. Dennis Hopper bobbed his head and sang a song to himself (although the film had no sound). Pop artist James Rosenquist sat on a twirling stool, his head popping in and out of the movie frame. Others barely moved.

These Screen Tests might be mistaken for a video of a photograph until a twitching smile or a blinking eye lets us know otherwise. Andy shot about five hundred of these Screen Tests between 1964 and 1966. Everyone who was anyone in New York, from society matrons to artists, rock musicians, and movie actors, wanted to make one. Some were used as backgrounds for Gerard Malanga's poetry readings, became part of Andy's multimedia shows, or were inserted into other Warhol movies. Most were seen once and filed away. Viewed today, they suggest an artistic relationship with Andy's photo booth and celebrity silk screens.

In the midst of the Factory's nonstop action Andy presided, passively encouraging his followers to compete for his attention and affection. Pat Hackett, who became one of his closest associates, said that Andy had been a late bloomer who spent his energy on work, not relationships. She explained that some of the power games he played were a kind of delayed adolescence, and she blithely compared him to a high school girl who suddenly finds herself popular— "creating cliques and setting up rivalries just for the entertainment value of watching people fight for his attention."

Andy's view of his life was different. "I'm just doing work. Doing things. Keeping busy. I think that's the best thing in life—keeping busy." He surrounded himself with people to help him with his mission. Andy's followers often speculated about why Andy wielded so much power over them. How did he get them to take care of things for him? Perhaps it stemmed from being the youngest child, the baby of the family, protected by his older brothers, petted by his mother, and treated as special by his father. The adored child, Andy retained a sense of entitlement that stayed with him for the rest of his life.

In her book *Famous for Fifteen Minutes,* Ultra Violet puzzled over Andy's amazing ability to mobilize so many talented people to work for free. She decided part of it was the exhilaration of being the in-crowd at the Factory, where art history was being made. Plus, she said, "I feel wonderfully liberated among the iconoclasts around him, for we are all equal— there are no saints, no sinners among us, no one is making judgments. We are free to be our worst selves or our best selves. And if that weren't joy enough, we are in the movies!"

The only person Andy paid a regular (if small) salary to was Gerard Malanga, his assistant in the studio. The rest waited for occasional handouts, hopeful that their association with Warhol would boost their own creative lives. Some had allowances from home. Others, like Billy Name, claimed that the sixties were about being bohemian, living for the moment. Billy said he didn't care about money or need it. There was always someone to foot the bill. Later there would be fights and lawsuits by disgruntled workers at the Factory who appeared in films or assisted in one capacity or another but never were paid.

Those who tired of Andy's promises that didn't materialize called him a Svengali, a manipulator, a voyeur. "It was a rough democracy," said art critic Dave Hickey. "A lot of people had their hearts broken. Andy fueled his career on the darker impulses of people." When Billy's roommate Freddie Herko, an out-of-work dancer and drug addict, committed suicide by jumping out of a window, Andy's reported response was "Why didn't he tell me? We could have gone down there and filmed it." Around town people called his reaction heartless and cold. His supporters said it was Andy's way of stepping back from the pain.

Perhaps sensing that Andy needed a shift from gloomy subjects and thoughts of death, Henry Geldzahler told him, "Enough death and disaster. Time for some life." Andy asked what he meant. Henry picked up a magazine lying around the Factory and pointed to some flowers. What could be more banal than flowers? Andy got right to work. He found a photograph of seven hibiscus blossoms in an issue of *Modern Photography,* which he altered by cutting off the stem and three of the blossoms and rotating the remaining four to fit on a square format. He sent the refigured flower image out to be converted into silk screens of various sizes.

During a two-month period, he and fifteen assistants turned out more than nine hundred flowers. The paintings, many in bright Day-Glo colors, look very little like the photograph. There is such a contrast between the black background and the brightly colored flowers that they seem to float in space. Some people thought the flowers were poppies because the silk screen process flattened the petals.

Dedicating the white flower paintings to Freddie Herko, Andy filled the Leo Castelli Gallery with the new Flower Series for his first show there in November 1964. A portrait of Jackie hung in the office, paying tribute to the first anniversary of JFK's death. The upbeat exhibit was a hit, both critically and in terms of sales. Ivan Karp was jubilant. "Andy is in a sense a victim of common things," he told an interviewer. "He genuinely admires them. How can you describe him? He's like a saint. Saint Andrew."

In the space of sixteen months, Andy had gone from an aspiring artist to a cause célèbre with the Most Wanted Men Series, the Brillo Boxes, the film award, and now the sensational Flower paintings.

In the ever more loose and decadent Factory atmosphere, Andy had his first brush with real violence. A friend of Billy and Ondine's arrived dressed in black leather, her Great Dane in tow, and asked if she could shoot his Marilyn paintings.

"Sure," said Andy.

With that she took off her white gloves, pulled a small pistol out of her pocket, shot a hole through a stack of Marilyns, and left.

Andy was shocked. "She shot my paintings!"

"Well," said Ondine, "you said she could."

Andy had probably expected her to use a camera, not a gun, but when he got over his surprise, he repaired the wounded works, retitling them *Shot Red Marilyn* and *Shot Blue Marilyn,* and sold them. Ondine said that Andy had no street smarts, no clue that he was courting disaster in allowing potentially violent people such easy access. He manipulated and provoked everyone around him to do more, try more, while he watched, cross-legged, his arms wrapped around him. Eventually it would backfire.

Poor Little Rich Girl   1965

The two girls I used most in my films, Baby Jane Holzer and Edie Sedgwick, are not representatives of current trends in women or fashion or anything. They're just used because they're remarkable in themselves. —Andy Warhol

At the beginning of 1965 another flower entered his life—a flower child named Edie Sedgwick. *Lovely, innocent, spoiled, vulnerable,* and *electric* are just some of the adjectives used to describe her. The twenty-one-year-old free spirit, fresh from a stay at Silver Hill, an expensive psychiatric hospital, and scarred by the first of two brothers' deaths, moved into her grandmother's Park Avenue apartment. A sometime art student who had "the best legs in New York," Edie aspired to be a model. Andy crossed paths with Edie at a party and hit her with his best line: "Come by the Factory. We'll put you in a movie."

Edie came from an old-money, East Coast WASP background by way of California. With Edie on his arm, Andy was invited into a new milieu of upper-crust parties, welcomed by people who would have snubbed him without her entrée. In turn, Andy offered Edie the opportunity to do something with her life other than halfheartedly study art and go out at night. "Very soon," he said, "Edie would be innovating her own look that *Vogue, Life,* and *Time* and all the other magazines would photograph—long, long earrings with dime store t-shirts over dancer's tights with a white mink coat thrown over it all."

He put her in his movies, where she soon eclipsed other Superstars, such as Baby Jane Holzer and Ultra Violet. Cutting her dark hair short and bleaching it silver to match Andy's, Edie became inseparable from him. They even dressed alike in matching striped jerseys, their faces pale with white makeup. Like Andy, Edie had a childlike quality. In her company, Andy felt like a "beauty" himself, a sentiment that until then had eluded him.

Edie's first film appearance was a nonspeaking part in *Vinyl.* It went so well that Andy gave her a starring role in the aptly titled *Poor Little Rich Girl,* an ironic echo of his childhood infatuation with Shirley Temple. It begins with an out-of-focus reel in which Edie talks about her privileged but misspent youth. Andy said, "Edie was incredible on camera—just the way she moved . . . she was all energy—she didn't know what to do with it when it came to living her life, but it was wonderful to film."

In *Beauty #2,* after viewing thirty-three unscripted minutes of Edie talking with two admirers as she lounged on the bed in her apartment, some thought the Doberman pinscher named Horse, who tried to jump off the bed and out of the film, was the only sensible one. This didn't stop the press from crowning Edie the underground film queen and toast of New York.

"Glamour she inhales. Glamour she exhales," said Ultra

Violet, who wrote that she paid several visits to Edie and tried to convince her to stop doing drugs. Everybody wanted to save Edie, though no one knew how.

"You just fell in love with her," said one admirer. "No matter what . . . if you were gay or straight . . . she was so beautiful, and so helpless and so rich and so bananas."

In May 1965 Andy took Edie to Paris for the opening of the Flower Series at the Sonnabend Gallery. He hoped to make a big splash there, and he and Edie were deluged by photographers and by invitations to parties and nightclubs. The show exceeded all expectations. And then, at the height of his success, Andy stunned the art world by announcing his intention to retire from painting. He was going to concentrate on moviemaking. "Art," he wrote later, "just wasn't fun for me anymore."

In Paris and New York, young girls imitated Edie's style, dressing in miniskirts, long dangling earrings, and high white boots. Her picture was plastered all over the gossip columns. All the publicity made her famous, but she wasn't earning any money, and her parents, increasingly upset by the details of her lifestyle, cut her allowance. Edie's friends then convinced her that Andy was taking advantage of her talent. They told her she could be a Hollywood star, even though she had never taken an acting lesson in her life. This prompted Edie to demand that she be paid for her work. She claimed that Andy was making a fool of her. In defense, Andy replied that the films were art and that he didn't make any money from them either. So how could he afford to pay her or anyone else?

Tired of Edie's histrionics and hurt that she didn't trust him, Andy went off to Fire Island to make a movie without her. He brought along Paul Morrissey, a young independent filmmaker, for technical assistance. Integrating sound and a moving camera, the film, titled *My Hustler,* starred a young discovery who was given the Factory name of Paul America, referring to his pinup-boy physique. He played the fledgling hustler who, in the sketchy story line, is pulled between two male would-be protectors. "*My Hustler* was the first full-length film to take a look at the lavender side of life without pointing a finger in disgust or disdain," said Normale, author of *Homosexual Action Movies*. To Edie's dismay, the film captured a wide audience and received good reviews.

Despite the falling-out between Andy and Edie, she accompanied him to his first one-man museum show at the Institute of Contemporary Art in Philadelphia. When they arrived at the opening in a limousine, a mob scene greeted them. Sam Green, the forward-looking director and an old friend of Andy's, had decorated the museum to look like the silver Factory. Word had spread that Factory Superstars would be there, and two thousand people, mostly students, showed up.

Edie, in a floor-length pink designer T-shirt dress, and Andy, clad all in black and hiding behind his signature wraparound sunglasses, found themselves surrounded by screaming, adoring fans. The security police hustled them past the stampeding hordes up to a balcony. From there they looked down on the crowd, who were chanting, "We want Andy and Edie!" Edie leaned over the balcony, microphone in hand, and, dangling her long pink sleeves just above their heads, cried, "Isn't Andy Warhol wonderful!"

Andy loved being treated with the adulation usually reserved for rock stars. "We weren't just at the art exhibit. We *were* the exhibit," he said. The rest of his friends, among them Leo Castelli, Ivan Karp, and Gerard Malanga, feared for their safety on the rickety balcony. The group finally escaped—breaking through a sealed door and scrambling down the fire escape and into waiting police cars. Sam Green, who worried that the opening would be frenzied, had all the paintings, except for a few Flowers, taken off the walls. The story that hit the papers crowned Andy and Edie's notoriety. Andy said he was glad he was making movies, as no one cared whether the art was on the walls or not.

Back in New York, what remained of the relationship between Edie and Andy disintegrated. When musician Bob Dylan's manager suggested that Edie might get a recording contract, she left the Factory for good. Seven years later, when she was only twenty-eight, the always at-risk young woman had burned out. She died of a drug overdose in California.

Many people blamed Andy for her drug addiction and tragic death. Yet Andy never overtly supported the use of drugs. It was not his nature to take an active part in the drama of someone else's life. In fact, the more he was pushed, the farther back he stood. "Now and then people would accuse me of being evil—of letting people destroy themselves while I watched, just so I could film or tape record them," Andy said. "But I learned when I was little that whenever I got aggressive and tried to tell someone what to do, nothing happened. I just couldn't carry it off." According to Andy, people did what they wanted to do, no matter what you told them. "You can't make them change if they don't want to—just like when they do want to, you can't stop them."

Andy was sorry to see Edie go, but he took her departure philosophically. He never pursued people who left him. And there were always new faces, such as Paul Morrissey, to supplant the old. Thanks to Morrissey's expertise in the technical and business aspects of filmmaking, he soon took on the central role in Andy's moviemaking schemes. The films Morrissey produced contained more of a story line than was usual at the Factory, although they still depended on improvisation and lengthy, unscripted conversation.

Like many other Factory regulars, including Brigid, Gerard, Ondine, Billy, and Andy himself, Paul Morrissey came from a Catholic background. Full of opinions, and a nonstop talker, Morrissey disliked drug users, abstract art, rock music, and new poetry. He called drug users and rock stars slimebags. His tough-guy act was in sharp contrast to Edie's needy fragility. Someone described Morrissey as "an extreme prude making X-rated movies." He possessed a strong enough personality to withstand the pressure-cooker atmosphere at the Factory and turned into a permanent fixture there. Some, like Edie, were not so lucky.

The Velvet Underground 1966

Publicity is like eating peanuts, once you start you can't stop. —Andy Warhol

One night, Andy and his entourage went to Café Bizarre in Greenwich Village to check out a band called the Velvet Underground. The hostile Velvets often played with their backs turned toward the audience. Their music was so repetitive and loud that all but the most die-hard customers fled. The Velvets were about to get fired. Andy called their act "fabulous and demented" and immediately invited them to come to the Factory.

Andy decided that, along with movies and the books he "wrote" with his tape recorder, the Factory ought to sponsor a multimedia event, a new phenomenon in the sixties. He'd been looking for a rock band that could perform while his films flashed on screens behind them. The Velvets seemed made to order—on the fringe enough to be hip, and so little known they would work for practically nothing. Songwriter and rhythm guitarist Lou Reed sang with a sweet-faced drummer, an electric-viola player, and a lead guitarist. Soon the Velvets were practicing at the Factory with their drums, tambourine, harmonica, guitars, and kazoos.

After listening to the cacophony for a few weeks, Andy concluded that the Velvets needed a female vocalist to make their act more appealing. He recently had met a singer and model named Nico. The young woman was a statuesque Viking with long blond hair and high cheekbones, fresh from Germany. Withdrawn, slightly depressed, she provided a total contrast to the chatty, gregarious Edie and Baby Jane. Andy admitted that her monotone sounded like "wind in a drainpipe" and that her halting singing style didn't blend with the deafening noise of the Velvets. Nevertheless, she would be his new Girl of the Year, mysterious and European, "a real moon goddess type."

One of the first opportunities for Andy and the Velvets to play together came from an unlikely source. Uncharacteristically, Andy accepted an invitation to speak at a meeting of the New York Society of Clinical Psychologists. He brought the band and some of his gang along to stage a performance instead. Nico bleated into the microphone and Gerard go-go danced, snapping a whip while the Velvets played against a backdrop of Warhol films. Barbara Rubin, a filmmaker, harassed the doctors with her microphone, asking them embarrassing questions about their sex lives. Many abruptly left their half-eaten dinners. The headline in the *Herald Tribune* the next day read "Psychiatrists Flee Warhol."

Why did this distinguished group invite Warhol, whose antics were public knowledge? Possibly because Andy was the embodiment of everything the 1960s wanted to be: cool. The old order was about class, money, and culture. The new order, with New York intellectuals inviting the Black Panthers for cocktails, wanted to break down social barriers. Radical chic, the writer Tom Wolfe called it. It was no wonder that the psychologists were eager to observe Andy Warhol, even though they were appalled by his shenanigans.

Andy had bigger plans for the Velvets than freaking out a group of doctors. The ad he placed in the *Village Voice* announced:

COME BLOW YOUR MIND
The Silver Dream Factory Presents
The Exploding Plastic Inevitable
with
Andy Warhol
The Velvet Underground
and
Nico.

For a month at a dance hall called the Dom, Andy staged an extravaganza complete with slides, movies, dancing, live music, and a strobe-light show. No one at that time had seen anything like it. People flocked to the Dom—uptown doyennes in long gowns, downtown hipsters in miniskirts and white boots, men in tie-dyed T-shirts and bell-bottoms, and a random crowd, both eclectically dressed and undressed. All in attendance gyrated frenetically in the huge darkened hall, lit only by the pulsating light show. Andy stood on the balcony running the slide projectors, working the lights, changing the colors. Gerard Malanga, Ingrid Superstar, Ondine, and various other Superstars put on a floor show. Their chief aim was entertaining Andy, whom they renamed Drella (a combination of Dracula and Cinderella).

After this gig, Andy took his show on the road with high hopes of a hit album and sold-out performances. Despite the notoriety and crowds, his efforts at a moneymaking endeavor never materialized. Nearly six months later, plagued by squabbles among the performers, canceled appearances, and rising costs, Andy's venture into rock and roll fizzled out. But the Velvets, along with the Rolling Stones, the Grateful Dead, and Bob Dylan, took their place as part of the history of rock music in the sixties.

For Andy, the failure of the Velvet Underground represented more than a financial loss. Realistic or not, money worries plagued him throughout his career. Henry Geldzahler explained, "There was an aching poverty early on, which hit [Andy] like a ton of bricks, and he just has never been on to, ah, experiencing that again. Even now he doesn't judge his success by the amount of money that is in various bank accounts or by the total value of his collection. He judges his success each year on how much money is coming in that year because underneath is always the image of total starvation and poverty and being evicted. There's no way he's ever going to get over that. . . . And what looks like cynicism to us, is really panic, I think." In addition, one of the reasons Andy needed to "bring home the bacon," as he said, was to continue to finance his unprofitable movies and feed his ever-present entourage.

Unfortunately, his artwork did not boost his finances. His latest show at Leo Castelli's, which coincided with the Dom events, featured his garish Day-Glo Cow Wallpaper and silver balloons that floated around the space like clouds. Nothing to buy but balloons. Yet the audience could participate by moving through the plump silver pillows. (Participatory Art was a new but short-lived movement in the sixties.) Andy, the compulsive collector, said people were burdened with too many objects. If you opened a window, the balloons could just glide away. The avant-garde choreographer Merce Cunningham used the balloons as a stage set for one of his dances, but the dancers kept bumping into them, so he ended up tying them down.

Andy was further discouraged about his art when Henry Geldzahler, who had been appointed curator of the prestigious Venice Biennale, failed to include him. Henry feared Andy would show up with his crew of exhibitionists and make an unfortunate scene. Andy never got over what he viewed as his good friend's betrayal. Yet, undeterred, Andy decided what he needed to do next: a blockbuster movie! He was convinced that his next film, however bizarre, would attain box office appeal.

Chelsea Girls   1966

Scripts bore me. It's much more exciting not to know what's going to happen. —Andy Warhol

The Chelsea Hotel. The historic luxury hotel, fallen on hard times, was home away from home to many artists, musicians, and writers, including Bob Dylan, Janis Joplin, Jimi Hendrix, and some of Andy's Superstars. That made it the perfect venue for Andy's next film, *Chelsea Girls*. The poet and songwriter Leonard Cohen said about the Chelsea, "I love hotels to which at four a.m. you can bring along a midget, a bear, and four ladies, drag them to your room and no one cares about it at all." Certainly no one paid any attention to the film crew running up and down the halls, in and out of rooms.

Typically, the camera rolled and the actors improvised according to sketchy suggestions from Andy or Paul Morrissey. Since most of the cast had been in previous Warhol films, they knew what was expected: talk and more talk, until their barest emotions came through. No matter that the batteries on the camera were running low and the sound was uneven; the show must go on. The vignettes (each thirty-three minutes long, the length of a reel of film) involved one or two actors in a hotel room, at the Factory, or at an apartment. In loud harangues, they sounded off until one of them broke down or the film ran out. Morrissey and Andy stirred the pot by inciting battles and competition between the actors before the shooting. Nerves on edge, already angry, with drug problems or other personal demons to fight, they were primed to explode.

In one scene, Ondine, playing the Pope, blew up at a young actress, pummeling her physically and verbally until she ran off crying. "You fool," he yelled after her. "You phony. Stop the camera"—along with choice expletives as he, too, left the set. The camera kept rolling. Brigid threw herself into the role of a lesbian drug dealer. Nico cut her bangs and cried. An actress playing Gerard's mother berated him for being a worthless hippie. An actor stood in front of the camera undressing and telling his life story. Only after many of the segments had been shot did Warhol tie the film together with a rough story line about a disparate group of residents in the Chelsea Hotel.

Running six and a half hours, with fifteen sequences, *Chelsea Girls* was too long to show in a theater, so Andy divided the footage into two films, running them side by side on a split screen. Color alternating with black-and-white, sound going on and off on one screen, then the other, emotional dramas—*Chelsea Girls* had a harrowing visual impact.

It opened in September 1966 at the Cinémathèque in New York, drawing sizeable audiences and ultimately achieving financial success—the first of Andy's movies to make money.

Hailed as the ultimate film of the sixties, for many conservatives it epitomized the degeneration of American culture. Today Warhol films can be seen as a precursor of reality TV and talk shows, where participants working without a script abandon any lingering inhibitions and get crazy for the camera. Andy would have relished every revealing, sordid moment.

Torn between glee and dismay, Brigid Berlin reported that after her very proper mother, Honey, had read a review of *Chelsea Girls* in *Time,* she disguised herself with a scarf and sunglasses and descended into the basement theater to see whether the reports of her daughter's wayward performance were true. Her worst fears were confirmed. She found *Chelsea Girls* mortifying, but to others, Andy's films reflected the real world far better—if more chaotically—than films put out by Hollywood.

Andy said, "Those movies showed you how some people act and react with other people. They were like actual sociological 'for instances.' They were like documentaries, and if you thought it could apply to you, it was an example." The film, with its desperate and disaffected characters, reflected a country in turmoil, a culture of changing values, but for some young viewers it was far more honest than the artificial world reflected by Hollywood. It also exposed the reckless and dangerous atmosphere around Andy.

Andy and "the kids," as he called them, had found a new hangout, a restaurant across the street from the Factory. Max's Kansas City, at Park Avenue South and 17th Street, was an all-night hangout for artists and musicians, including the Warhol Factory regulars. In the front room, artists who were or would be important in the next few years—including Robert Rauschenberg, John Chamberlain, and Chuck

Close—sprawled against the bar. In the middle room sat the music heavies—Mick Jagger, Bob Dylan, Jimi Hendrix. In the back room Andy held court. Owner Mickey Ruskin said, "If I liked somebody they had an absolute right to do whatever they wanted." Andy arranged to trade Mickey artwork in return for bill-signing privileges for his posse. And they made Max's a wild scene. Jimi Hendrix said, "Max's Kansas City was where you could let your freak flag fly." The back room at Max's was certainly no place for the squeamish or faint-hearted.

Chelsea Girls opened in various theaters around the country. It was surprising, considering the X-rated content, that more cities did not close it down. To capitalize on the film's success, Paul Morrissey released some of Andy's earlier films, which played to disappointed audiences. The prestigious Cannes Film Festival invited Andy to screen *Chelsea Girls,* but when he and his entourage arrived at the French seaside resort town, they learned that the screening had been canceled by the French film board, which feared a controversy. Still, Andy hung around, meeting such celebrities as French actress Brigitte Bardot, whose portrait he later painted.

In the fall, the Institute of Contemporary Art in Boston exhibited for the first time a new series, Self-Portraits. Appearing in various lurid color combinations, Andy looks passively out at the viewer, his finger to his mouth, his face half hidden, the cool voyeur offering no hint of his feelings. Clarity of vision is reserved for the artist looking out, rather than the viewer looking in. However, the blotches of bubbling color spilling out from his brain suggest an inner turmoil the artist might have preferred to camouflage.

Enter Fred Hughes   1967

*You get to the point in life where you're actually invited to the
party of parties . . . and it still didn't guarantee that you wouldn't feel like a
complete dud! —Andy Warhol*

Students streamed into the campus auditorium. Although
most of them had never seen a Warhol film, they flocked to
Andy's lecture because he was famous. It was 1967, and to
make some extra money, Paul Morrissey, Andy, and his new
Girl of the Year, the actress and writer Viva, were traveling
around to college campuses. Andy introduced his road show
by running a segment from one of his most boring films.

Clad in a leather jacket and dark glasses, he stood on the
stage at this Midwestern university, looking out and passively
silent. Then Paul delivered a tirade against art films, hippies,
and marijuana in fast-paced, intellectual banter. Afterward
Viva fielded questions, advising the audience to drop out of
school and subvert authority. The students, unimpressed and

getting belligerent, responded by hissing and booing. For this, Andy's fee was $1,000 per lecture.

After several such dismal events, Andy, fed up and worried about being away from the Factory and his increasingly frail mother, hired an out-of-work actor to impersonate him for the next four campus visits. The actor's name was Alan Midgette, and with his part-Cherokee heritage, he looked nothing like Andy. Still, he slathered himself with the palest shade of Erase cover stick, donned a silver wig, and answered questions in quintessential Warholian monosyllables.

The ruse was exposed when he stepped off a plane and the wig blew off. Andy said, "Uh, well, we just did it, well. I, oh, because, uh, I don't really have that much to say. The person who went had so much more to say. He was better at it than I am." After Andy died, Alan Midgette would turn up at art openings dressed as Andy, and people would greet him, saying, "Oh, Andy, we're so glad you're back."

Meanwhile at the Factory, a few dangerous episodes took place, including a holdup by two Union Square drug addicts. Many of Andy's Superstars, who had never been paid for their film work, were disillusioned. And in spite of the success of *Chelsea Girls,* filmmaking continued to be a drain on Andy's bank account. To make matters worse, Andy Warhol Enterprises was in financial disarray, and lately because of a slowdown in the economy, the Castelli Gallery had not been successful in selling Andy's artwork.

Into the disorder entered a young Texan named Fred Hughes. As a representative for the de Menils, a great art-collecting dynasty in Houston, Fred had developed a good eye for art. Small-boned and slim, with black hair slicked back, he spoke with a patrician accent and dressed like an aristocrat in custom-made suits, silk cravats, and handmade loafers. To top off his look, he sported a black ten-gallon hat. Occasionally he implied that he was related to the reclusive billionaire Howard Hughes. In actuality, his father had been a traveling salesman, and he had been brought up in ordinary circumstances. But Andy, who had transformed himself, never minded self-invention. He recognized Fred's talents immediately and was relieved to turn his business over to him. Fred's ability to charm the rich, combined with his biting wit, appealed to Andy. "I'm deeply superficial," Fred often said, boasting that he had memorized the names of all the kings and queens of England and the style of chair that went with them.

"Fred," Andy said, "is really up there"—his euphemism for social climbing. He especially welcomed Fred's access to the de Menil fortune. On one of Fred's first ventures, he took John and Dominique de Menil and Andy to Expo '67 in Montreal, where Andy's six-foot-square Self-Portraits hung alongside works of many of America's top painters. Not long afterward the de Menils commissioned Andy to do a film of sunsets. These reels eventually ended up in his film **** (*Four Stars*), which lasted twenty-four hours. The cast was identical to that of *Chelsea Girls,* with everyone bantering, but presented more as images in a tapestry of color and form.

Around this time Fred Hughes offered a job to a young telegram deliveryman, telling him that they wouldn't pay more than Western Union but at least he could work in one place all day. A native of Los Angeles, Jed Johnson appealed to Fred's taste for refinement and Andy's taste for "beauties." Like most young men at the Factory, Jed started out sweeping floors, but he had more to offer. Quiet, unassuming, and dependable, he moved gracefully between assisting in film direction and doing odd jobs. It also seemed as if Andy had found the perfect boyfriend, and for the moment, Andy's life seemed in good hands.

With Fred managing the sale of his artwork, Andy had the cash to continue his filmmaking ventures. He was determined to make a big-screen hit movie, and he and Morrissey planned to film a Western, completely in the great outdoors. The cast gathered in Oracle, Arizona, for a five-day location shoot. They ignored the two-paged typed outline, supposedly for a Wild West *Romeo and Juliet,* that passed for a script. Instead the film became an ode to the old West; they titled it *Lonesome Cowboys*. It starred Viva, who played the operator of a dance hall and bordello, and her Romeo, a handsome young California surfer named Tom Hompertz, whom Andy had discovered on their lecture tour at San Diego State College.

From the beginning things did not go well. Several cast members failed to turn up. Drag queens dressed as cowboys, who shared makeup tips and bun-tightening ballet exercises at the hitching rail, offended the good folks of Oracle. A group of gawking tourists, horrified by a simulated rape scene in which Viva was accosted by the "cowboys," called the local sheriff, who thereafter did regular drive-bys, though no one knew for sure whether he wanted to arrest someone or be in the movie. One of the construction crew expressed his critical opinion by hammering continuously during the shooting.

Andy, realizing the film was doomed, remarked, "Maybe I should just shoot a cactus for thirty-five minutes. If we have to think about art, a cactus is the most beautiful piece of sculpture around." After Viva protested that a local cowboy had ruined one of her lines by driving his Jeep onto the set, Andy bluntly said, "Your line was no good anyway." Then the

FBI heard that Andy was making an obscene film and started a dossier on him. They shadowed both Andy and his film distributors for months. Although *Lonesome Cowboys* did not turn out to be the hoped-for blockbuster, it is one of Andy's most famous films.

Yet at the time the reviews were merciless. *Time* wrote: "Now that Boris Karloff and Bela Lugosi have passed on, Viva! stands unrivaled as the screen's foremost purveyor of horror. By the simple expedient of removing her clothing, she can produce a sense of primordial terror several nightmares removed from any mad doctor's laboratory." But by the time the movie came out, Andy had worse problems than a few bad reviews.

Shot! 1968

I was in the wrong place at the right time. —Andy Warhol

100

She looked harmless. Bundled up in a coat and turtleneck sweater in spite of the warm June weather, she waited on the sidewalk for Andy to arrive. In her hand was a crumpled paper bag. Valerie Solanas, hopeful filmmaker, radical feminist, and founder and sole member of SCUM, the Society for Cutting Up Men, had once sent Andy a screenplay, but even he found it extreme. "It was so dirty I suddenly thought she might be working for the police department and that this was some kind of entrapment." He lost the script, but when Valerie telephoned him, believing he'd stolen it, and demanded money to pay her rent, he offered her twenty-five dollars for a day's work in *I, a Man,* the film they were shooting that day. The experience seemed to placate her. Afterward she only called Andy occasionally to give her man-hating rap about plans for "an out-of-sight, groovy, all-female world."

When Andy and Jed Johnson encountered Valerie that summer day, she accompanied them up to the third floor of the Factory. Paul Morrissey sat at one of the two reception-area desks, talking on the telephone to Viva. He told Andy that Viva was uptown having her hair dyed for a small role in the Hollywood movie *Midnight Cowboy*.

At the other desk sat Fred Hughes, now president of Andy Warhol Enterprises, waiting with Mario Amaya, an art critic and curator, to discuss an upcoming London retrospective with Andy. It was all business as usual.

Then Valerie reached into her crumpled paper bag and pulled out a .32 caliber pistol. She pointed it at Andy. He paid no attention until she fired.

The first shot missed. Andy leaped to his feet. "No! No! Valerie! Don't do it!" She fired again. Andy fell to the floor under the desk, trying to crawl away. She reached down to fire a third time. The bullet entered Andy's side and came out his back. Blood poured onto the floor.

Valerie charged on. Across the room Mario Amaya crouched on the floor. He thought a sniper was shooting at them from across the street. Valerie fired at him, missed, then shot again, grazing his hip. He ran into the back room. Billy Name, who had been working in the darkroom, found him leaning against the door, holding it shut, dripping blood. "Valerie shot Andy," Mario rasped.

Meanwhile, Valerie turned her gun on Fred. He fell to his knees. "Please don't shoot me, Valerie," he begged. "I'm innocent. Just leave." She pushed the elevator button to go down, then pressed the gun to Fred's forehead. The elevator arrived, and Fred again pleaded, "You better get out of here right away." Valerie got on the elevator. The doors shut behind her.

Fred sped into action. He rushed over to give the gasping Andy mouth-to-mouth resuscitation. But Andy asked him to stop because it made him feel worse. Then someone shouted to call the police and an ambulance. Billy leaned over Andy, who whispered, "Oh, please don't make me laugh, Billy. Please. It hurts too much."

Billy held Andy's head tenderly. "I'm not laughing, Andy. I'm crying."

It took fifteen minutes for the emergency medical services to reach the Factory. The stretcher wouldn't fit into the elevator, so they carried Andy down the steep, narrow stairwell. The wounded Mario Amaya lay in the ambulance next to the unconscious Andy. "For an extra fifteen dollars, we can turn on the siren," said the driver.

"Turn it on," said Mario. "Leo Castelli will pay."

At 4:45 p.m. Andy arrived at the emergency room of Columbus Hospital–Cabrini Medical Center. A team had been alerted to stand by, but twenty-three minutes had passed since the shooting. They examined the bleeding artist. "Forget it," someone muttered. "No chance." At 4:51 Andy was pronounced dead.

Mario heard them. He sat up on his stretcher, where he was waiting his turn. "It's Andy Warhol," he shouted. "He's famous. And he's rich. . . . Do something!"

The doctors ripped Andy's chest open to massage his heart, then sent him up to surgery. The operation lasted more than five hours. The bullets had nicked a pulmonary artery and passed through vital organs before exiting, leaving a big hole in his chest. Andy also had lost a great deal of blood.

As word of the shooting got out, Andy's art dealers and

Factory entourage gathered in the waiting room. Gerard Malanga brought Julia, who, as press cameras went off, was bundled into a wheelchair by the hospital staff. "Why did they shoot my Andy?" she wept.

She was the only one among the assembled crowd not interested in giving an interview. In one corner Ivan Karp and Leo Castelli talked to reporters. In another Viva and Ultra Violet held forth. Ultra later confessed to feeling a little self-conscious about using Andy's shooting for what she admitted could be taken for shameless self-promotion, but she comforted herself with the knowledge that Andy had made a silk screen of Marilyn Monroe the day after the actress's suicide. He had told her that timing was everything. Who understood better than he the craving for publicity?

Those who didn't stay at the hospital held vigil in their own way. Mario Amaya, whose wound turned out to be minor, got bandaged up and attended a dinner party. One of the Superstars threatened to throw herself out the window if Andy died, and kept demanding bulletins from the hospital. Nico and the Superstar International Velvet lit candles, pulled the curtains, and meditated until they heard that Andy was out of surgery.

That evening Valerie Solanas turned herself in to a traffic policeman in Times Square. When word of her arrest reached the police station, Fred Hughes and Jed Johnson, who had been held on suspicion, were released. Valerie insisted she had been right to shoot Andy. "He had too much control over my life," she declared.

The newspapers carried headlines about the Warhol shooting, but the editorials were not very sympathetic. They tended to blame Andy, holding him personally responsible for the excesses of the sixties. *Time* said, "The Pop art king was the blond guru of a nightmare world, photographing depravity and calling it truth." And a *Daily News* columnist moralized, "Long before Valerie Solanas got around to pouring her venom at Andy Warhol through the muzzle of a gun, the waspish, silvery-haired Maharishi of Modness was in trouble, deep trouble. His world . . . suddenly stopped caring, stopped knowing, stopped even realizing that Andy Warhol was alive and reasonably well." Andy had a different view: "I can start things but I can't stop them."

The day after the shooting, Andy was pushed off the front pages by Senator Robert Kennedy's assassination in Los Angeles. Lying in the hospital, wavering in and out of semi-consciousness, Andy saw the Catholic funeral service on the television and thought *he* had died.

He stayed confined in the hospital for nearly two months. During this time Andy's nephews came from Pittsburgh to comfort Julia, who was hysterical with worry. Upon Andy's release, his brothers and their families tried to help, but they resented Jed Johnson's influence. Paul said his mother put Andy back together, not Jed, as those at the Factory assumed.

Eventually Andy went back to work, wearing a surgical corset to keep his insides in place. He joked that the ugly scars that slashed across his stomach and chest made his torso look like a Dior dress, and arranged for a close-up portrait by the famed photographer Richard Avedon. But there were other scars, deeper scars that didn't heal. For the first time, Andy realized the danger of the Factory's open-door policy. "The fear of getting shot again made me think that I'd never again enjoy talking to someone whose eyes look weird. But when I thought about that I got confused because it included almost everybody I really enjoyed."

Valerie Solanas's telephoned threats from jail amplified his fear. Yet Andy refused to testify at her trial. The court judged her mentally incompetent, sentencing her to three years in a mental hospital, with a year off for time served.

The Factory had started to change under the management of Fred Hughes, and now the changes accelerated. Fred told friends such as Ondine and Viva not to drop by without an appointment. And getting an appointment wasn't easy. Fred "hired" a series of well-born Europeans to answer the phones. That some of them barely spoke English didn't seem to matter. A receptionist fortified the entrance, and a buzzer was installed at the door.

Andy continued to feel afraid to be alone at the Factory; every time the elevator door opened, he flinched. Around this time he hired a young English major from Columbia, Pat Hackett, who soon became indispensable, both as a loyal confidante and as an intelligent transcriber of the audio tapes Andy religiously recorded at parties and on the telephone. Pat didn't drink or do drugs and led a discreet private life. "Andy expected everyone who worked for him to do their job, but he was nonetheless grateful when they did," she said. "He knew that any degree of conscientiousness was hard to find, even when you paid for it. . . . I never heard anyone say 'Thank you' more than Andy, and from his tone, you always felt he meant it."

Billy Name, feeling left out of this new Factory, retreated into the darkroom. He lived there, coming out only at night. Occasionally take-out food containers left by the door proved he was still around. Sometimes people heard him talking to himself or reading out loud, but when they tried to make contact he ignored their pleas.

Andy refused to do anything about it. He said he didn't

know what had made Billy take refuge in the darkroom, so how could he make him come out? One day in the spring of 1970 the door to the darkroom stood open. On the wall was a note—"Andy, I am not here but I am fine. Love Billy." In many ways it was the end of an era.

Interview   1969–1970

I hate subscriptions. If we fold I don't want to give the money back.
—Andy Warhol

The young Columbia University film student stood in front of the tenth-floor offices of *Interview,* the magazine Andy had launched so that he "could get press passes to movies." The doors of the fledgling magazine were locked and chained, and the editor and his assistant were nowhere in sight. Since the student, Bob Colacello, needed to turn in a freelance article, he went down to check out the sixth-floor studio. He found Andy sitting at his desk eating lunch. When he asked what was going on, Andy said vaguely, "Oh, uh, something happened," and added that Paul Morrissey wanted to talk to Bob.

To Bob's complete shock, Paul told him that the editor had been fired, and offered him a position. Paul told him, "Putting together a magazine isn't that big a deal. You just slap some pretty pictures down on the page." He also reasoned that Columbia might give Bob film course credits for taking the job. And since it was a part-time slot, Paul offered to pay forty dollars per week, slave wages even in 1970. Bob negotiated a ten-dollar raise and accepted the job.

Interview was a natural next step for Andy, who intuitively understood the concept of branding—developing a high-profile corporate identity to sell many different products—long before it became a business buzzword. Andy Warhol Enterprises, Andy believed, should include all media—art, movies, books, and a magazine to publicize these projects. Gerard Malanga said, "Andy wanted to be like Walt Disney. In other words the entrepreneur of 'Andy Warhol Presents.' " For inspiration Andy looked not to Mickey Mouse, but to two new magazines that in a short period had catapulted to the top. One, *Rolling Stone,* covered the music scene; the other, *Screw,* consistently pushed the boundaries of sexual publishing to new areas of vulgarity but obtained borderline respect by taking on many First Amendment issues. Always seizing trends and staying ahead of the curve, Andy said, "Let's combine the two ideas—kids and sex—and we'll make a fortune."

Debuting in November 1969, *Interview: A Monthly Film Journal* was a tabloid-size paper on cheap newsprint. The first cover featured Viva. Listed among the editors on the initial masthead were Andy, Gerard Malanga, and Paul Morrissey, who had taken over not only the filmmaking but also the day-to-day running of the Factory.

The magazine ran on a minuscule budget. For example, after the first issue was off the presses, Andy's lawyer discovered that an interviewee had referred to a well-known movie critic as a drag queen. The lawyer advised that calling the critic a drag queen was libelous but that just plain "queen" would be fine. Reprinting the whole issue, however, was too expensive for the fledgling publication, Pat Hackett said. "So Andy, Paul, Fred, Jed, Gerard, and I, plus whoever happened to walk in the door, spent about six hours sitting in the front of the loft going through bundle after bundle of *Interview*s and crossing out the word 'drag' with black felt-tip pens, while Morrissey complained, 'This is like doing penance—I will never call him a drag queen again, I will never call him a drag queen again. . . .'"

Andy's chief edict to Bob Colacello was "No poetry." Poetry, he said, was not "modern." Interviews conducted the Andy Warhol way, preferably stars interviewing stars, tape-recorded, transcribed, and then printed with all the *ah*s, *um*s, and *oh*s intact—that defined "modern." Andy brought his "wife, Sony" the tape recorder, everywhere, and as soon as anyone started talking, he whipped it out and pushed the On button. No editing necessary. Everybody sounded as they sounded. Andy wanted it to be "real." "The acquisition of my tape recorder really finished whatever emotional life I might have had," he said. "And I was glad to see it go."

He did at least one interview per issue, usually with someone famous. Bob always escorted Andy to these meetings. His role was to pose "important" questions while Andy fished for gossip. Bob said, "Talking to Andy, they thought, was like talking to a worshipful fan, not a reporter—but a fan who was also a star and therefore an equal. He asked such cute, harmless questions, like 'What's your favorite color?' The kind of questions a child might ask, not realizing that, as Sony rolled on relentlessly, these children's questions sometimes make adults look foolish."

Another of Andy's rules: "The interviews can be funny, but the pictures can't." He understood only too well that "almost everybody loves the sound of his or her own voice and almost nobody loves the way he or she looks." So the printers tweaked and airbrushed the photographs until everyone looked "glamorous," another pet Warhol word. Bob reassured the nervous that "we retouch anyone over the age of twenty."

The covers featured the young, the good-looking, and the hip, whether they were movie stars, musicians, or socialites. Covers of TV stars didn't sell, probably because *Interview* readers didn't watch television. They went to discos. Quickly *Interview* evolved from a film review magazine to a slick tabloid on fashion, art, music, and books. *Interview,* a precursor to *People,* turned people into celebrities, playing into the public's insatiable thirst for gossip.

After Andy was shot, Paul Morrissey took over much of the filmmaking, shifting the emphasis from Andy's looser, more artistic approach to stories with actual plots. Andy's name appeared over the title, but he generally stayed away from the day-to-day filming. The latest Warhol Superstar was Joe Dallesandro, a hunk with a biceps tattoo that said LITTLE JOE, referring to his small stature. Another working-class Catholic boy and a product of New York reform schools and foster homes, Dallesandro was a subdued contrast to the other shrieking, self-involved Superstars at the Factory. "In my movies, everyone's in love with Joe Dallesandro," said Andy.

Dallesandro appeared in *Lonesome Cowboys* and several other films, but his first starring role was in *Flesh,* the slice-of-life tale of a male hustler meeting various partners in the course of a day. Joe's sculptured torso mesmerized the audience. However, two of the bit players who stole the show in *Flesh* were the transvestite drag queens Jackie Curtis and

Candy Darling, who with Holly Woodlawn would become the new pop idols of Warhol's films. Valerie Solanas had left Andy with an abiding fear of the slightly off-the-wall women who had previously appealed to him, and perhaps to take their place he began to cast transvestites in women's roles. Andy told interviewer David Bailey that it wasn't really correct to call them drag queens, since drag queens were men who dressed up like women for part of the day, "whereas the people we use, think they really are women." Modeling their personas on Hollywood stars of the thirties and forties, Jackie Curtis was the tough, sexy dame with runs in her stockings and stubble showing through her makeup; Holly Woodlawn, who starred with Joe Dallesandro in the next Morrissey-Warhol movie, *Trash,* was the spunky, funny, streetwise minx; and Candy Darling was the platinum-blond beauty. In fact, Andy said, "Candy was the most striking drag queen I've ever seen. On a good day, you couldn't believe she was a man."

Part of the reason Andy let Paul Morrissey take over the filmmaking was that under his direction the movies were making money. Andy always emphasized the bottom line because, as he incessantly reminded his employees, "I have a lot of mouths to feed—someone has to bring home the bacon." This was also the reason he insisted that *Interview* be slanted toward the young, affluent population that advertisers wanted to reach. Andy suggested that all interviews mention as many brands as possible, preferably perfume, makeup, and jewelry, since those products advertised the most. Andy was one of the first to realize the effectiveness of product placement.

To keep costs down, Fred Hughes encouraged volunteer "interns." If someone from a Social Register family was willing to work for free, no one minded that he or she arrived late or couldn't type. Trying to get the magazine out with an English beer heiress copy editor who changed all the American spellings to British ones, or a six-foot-five intern who couldn't type and arrived for the first day of work wearing shorts and a pith helmet, all seemed part of the *Interview* challenge. In spite of—or because of—everything, the magazine attracted subscribers.

Whereas Warhol movies had been about freaks and homegrown superstars, *Interview* became Andy's conduit to a new kind of star—a heady mix of Hollywood, rock royalty, models, and international A-list types who Andy hoped could afford to come up with the $25,000 price of a portrait (plus $5,000 for each additional portrait). Andy also thought that since *Interview* wasn't actually making money (and it wouldn't until 1979), the magazine should promote more profitable areas of Andy Warhol Enterprises. Of these the biggest moneymakers were portraits.

Andy's procedure for making a portrait was elaborate. According to Pat Hackett, "It began with the subject posing while he took approximately sixty Polaroid photos. From those sixty shots he would choose four and give them to a screen printer. When those came back to him he would choose one image, decide where to crop it, and then doctor it cosmetically in order to make the subject appear as attractive as possible—he'd elongate necks, trim noses, enlarge lips, and clear up complexions as he saw fit. . . . Then he would have the cropped, doctored image on the 8" X 10" blown up to a 40" X 40" acetate, and from that the screen printer would make a silkscreen."

Andy kept a roll of painted canvas in the studio—one shade for men, another for women, to be ready for the portraits. However, if the purchaser wanted the background to be green to match their sofa or pink to pick up a fleck in their curtains, Andy was happy to oblige. The only thing he refused to change was the size—a 40" by 40" format. He had a plan not shared with the clients: Someday he would exhibit all of his portraits, hung side by side, along a huge gallery wall— the portrait of an age.

To meet possible clients for portrait commissions and to keep himself in the public eye, Andy often appeared with his entourage at two or three parties each evening before heading to a disco or club. He expected his staff to be constantly assessing potential clients. He often pulled Fred Hughes or Bob Colacello aside to nag, "Have you popped the question yet?" Anyone who landed a paying customer received a small percentage of the fee. Portraits varied from wealthy collectors to celebrities such as Imelda Marcos, notorious wife of the dictator of the Philippines; singer Liza Minnelli; President Jimmy Carter; boxing champion Muhammad Ali; even Andy's old crush Truman Capote.

Warhol portraits were like Warhol interviews—a star painting the portrait of a star, or a person wealthy enough to command the attention of one. In terms of art history, these paintings of the high and mighty continued a tradition of portrait painting dating back to fifteenth-century Europe, where the rich and the royal commissioned their likenesses.

Interview provided Andy with a new ploy to lure fresh faces to the Factory. He no longer offered to put people in movies. Instead, he asked them if they'd like to be in the magazine. Or, better yet, on the cover. As an opening gambit, it was hard to beat.

Putting My Andy On   1970–1974

I don't get too close. I don't like to touch things, that's why my work is so distant from myself. —Andy Warhol

Up at the town house on Lexington Avenue, Julia Warhola was lonely. She had begun her life in New York sleeping in the same room as her son, feeding dinner to his friends, working on his art, and often signing his drawings. Now Andy's travel schedule and frantic social life didn't leave much time for her, and though Jed Johnson lived in the town house, too, Andy never invited even his closest friends there. So when the photographer David Bailey came to interview Julia, she poured her heart out. She still hoped that somehow Andy would marry. "All those beautiful people coming in the house, all these boys," she said. "I wouldn't mind if he would really get engaged and marry one of the boys . . . maybe he would get a little baby, I mean a little Andy." Julia envisioned "all these little Andys, you know, Andys, Andys, Andys, Andys,

Andys . . . wouldn't that be beautiful?" She could have been visualizing one of her son's paintings, with its repeated images.

What seemed obvious to the people who did see Julia was that Mrs. Warhola had lost touch with reality. Sweet, soft-spoken Jed worried as her behavior became more erratic. Julia was prone to wandering out of the house, leaving the door open, and forgetting where she lived. She accused Jed of poisoning her food and spoke of imaginary disturbances in the wall of her bedroom. Not quite twenty years after Mrs. Warhola moved in with Andy, she went back for a visit to Pittsburgh, where she suffered a stroke. She never returned to New York.

Andy always preferred to eat Julia's plain home cooking before going out for the evening, and after her departure he often had dinner with his two housekeepers. He would stop at home, eat, and "glue," as he called it—cleaning up and choosing a wig for the night's events. He self-mockingly referred to this process as "putting my Andy on." Sometimes he changed his clothes and sprayed himself with perfume. On a spring evening in 1971, before the gala opening of his retrospective at the Whitney Museum, he hired a long black limousine and filled it with some of the old Factory regulars— among them Viva, Brigid, and Nico, costumed in beads and boas. The car pulled up at the Whitney to a satisfying flurry of flashbulbs and news cameras, and two more of Andy's Superstars, Candy Darling, in her platinum-blond bombshell drag, and Ultra Violet, in a see-through dress, swooped down, grabbing Andy's arms to be included in the photographs.

Andy had requested that the gallery walls of the Whitney be covered with his Cow Wallpaper, on which hung the paintings of soup cans, Marilyns, car crashes, electric chairs, and Jackies. The result was a triumph; even Andy's severest critics admitted it. John Canaday wrote in the *New York Times,* "The plain inescapable fact that will give pain to his enemies, is that Andy looks better than he has ever looked before." And Barbara Rose, writing in *New York,* called his paintings "fresh and brilliant."

In her long article, Rose also commented on Warhol's cultural relevance. "Andy does it again, turning the Whitney into a boutique covered with wallpaper of cows—the stock subject of popular academic middle-class paintings. Of course, the museum has been a boutique for a long time and people have been treating the paintings like wallpaper even longer, but Andy spells it out with his usual cruel clarity."

That same year Andy designed a cover for the new Rolling Stones album *Sticky Fingers*. The image shows a waist-to-midthigh close-up of a man in a pair of blue jeans, with a real zipper. Unzipped, it reveals a man in a pair of white Jockey shorts. Andy used the assignment as an excuse to take a number of photographs of different models for the cover and the inside shot. Many take credit for being the man on the *Sticky Fingers* album cover, but generally the vote goes to Jed Johnson in the blue jeans and to *Interview* editor Glenn O'Brien in the underwear. The album sold in the millions and today is a collector's item. Andy said if he ever designed another album cover, he should get a royalty on each album sold, not a flat fee.

To expand Andy's finances, Fred Hughes encouraged him to concentrate on his paintings. Andy's Swiss dealer, Bruno Bischofberger, thought Andy should paint a series on a world leader for an exhibit at his gallery. He suggested Albert Einstein. Andy thought Chairman Mao, the dictator of China, would be a better choice. "I've been reading so much about China. . . . The only picture they ever have is of Mao Zedong. It's great. It looks like a silkscreen," Andy said. Bruno insisted that no one, especially Americans, would buy them, since Mao was a widely hated Communist.

As usual, Andy trusted his instincts and set about silk-screening a set of prints, line drawings, and paintings of the Chinese leader. Mao symbolized power over the lives of a billion people. Of course, had Andy lived in Communist China during the Cultural Revolution, he probably would have been jailed. Mao suppressed creativity, especially in the arts. But Andy felt sure that capitalist American collectors would find the image of Chairman Mao, both alien and familiar at the same time, irresistible. And he was right on target.

Based on an official photograph of Mao, the portraits were done in a freer brushstroke than previous paintings, with a looser background of color over which the image of Mao was printed. By adding lines around the face for emphasis, Andy made the Communist leader as glamorous as his portraits of Marilyn. Then Andy produced wallpaper with Mao's plump head lined up like purple plums against a white background. At his 1974 exhibition in the Musée Galliera in Paris, the Mao paintings (more than two thousand) hung in long rows over the Mao wallpaper—a decorative and colorful display.

Andy followed his paintings of Chairman Mao with an edition of prints. There were several differences between the paintings and the prints. The former were silk-screened on canvas, the latter on paper. In the paintings, the artist worked on the surface by hand after the silk-screen process. The appearance of brushstrokes adds a stylish dimension and is reminiscent of Andy's early cartoon paintings. Both paintings and prints by Warhol came in limited editions, but the prints were made in quantity, up to 250 in one edition.

In 1972 Andy turned his attention to another government leader, this time an American, George McGovern. The Democratic candidate in the upcoming presidential election, McGovern was running against the Republican incumbent, Richard Nixon. To bolster McGovern's campaign finances, Andy made a print edition of Nixon's face in an unflattering pea green color. Underneath it he scrawled "Vote McGovern." The poster, which raised $42,000, managed to confuse voters as to which candidate it touted. Later Andy blamed the anti-Nixon poster for his yearly investigations by the Internal Revenue Service.

For a person who appeared to live most of his life in the public eye, Andy fiercely guarded his private life. In 1972, in a nursing home in Pittsburgh where she had been moved after a stroke, Julia died. Andy had continued to pay her bills, but he insisted that his brothers give their mother a modest funeral and refrain from putting an announcement in the newspapers. "Don't tell anyone," he warned them. Paul and John, who idolized their famous brother, followed his instructions. Even Andy's close friends and associates didn't know for several years of Julia's death. When they inquired how she was, Andy simply responded, "Fine. She doesn't get out much."

Andy went on as if nothing had happened. Preoccupied with painting again, he paid only minimal attention to the films that Paul Morrissey was producing and directing. The third in a trilogy starring Joe Dallesandro, *Heat* costarred noted New York actress Sylvia Miles. The film won critical praise (though New York critic Vincent Canby said he missed Holly Woodlawn, Candy Darling, Jackie Curtis, and Viva). *Heat* was

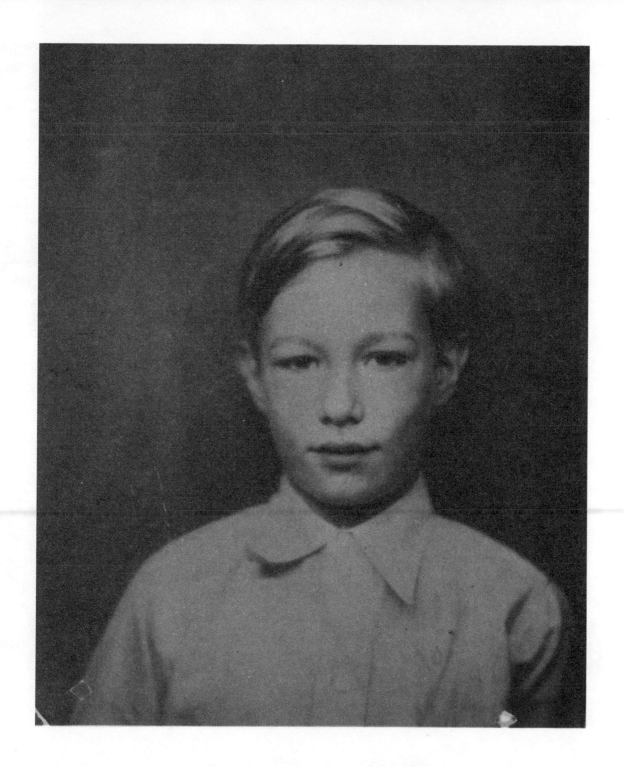

Andy Warhol, age eight, about 1936.
Founding Collection, Andy Warhol Museum, Pittsburgh.

Andy (center) around age fourteen, about 1942, with his brothers, Paul (left) and John (right).
Founding Collection, Andy Warhol Museum, Pittsburgh.

Andy (center) with his family in front of their home at 3252 Dawson Street, about 1947. From left to right: aunt Eva Bezek, mother Julia Warhola, brother John Warhola, Andy, and brother Paul Warhola, with children Paul Jr. and Eva.

Founding Collection, Andy Warhol Museum, Pittsburgh.

Untitled (cat from *25 Cats Name Sam and One Blue Pussy*), about 1954.
Offset lithograph, watercolor, and pen on paper. 9-1/8 x 6 in.

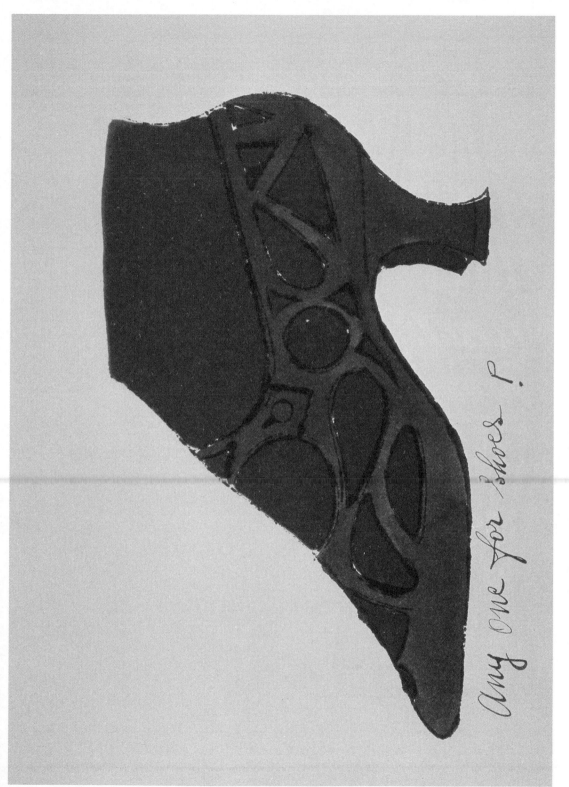

Anyone for Shoes? (from the portfolio A La Recherche du Shoe Perdu), 1955.
Offset lithography, watercolor, and pen on paper. 9-3/4 x 13-3/4 in.
© The Andy Warhol Foundation, Inc./Art Resource, NY. © 2004 Andy Warhol Foundation
for the Visual Arts, Artists Rights Society (ARS), NY.

Large Coca-Cola, **about 1962. Synthetic polymer paint on canvas. 85 x 57 in.**
© The Andy Warhol Foundation, Inc./Art Resource, NY. © 2004 Andy Warhol Foundation
for the Visual Arts, Artists Rights Society (ARS), NY.

Campbell's Soup Cans, 1962. **Thirty-two canvases: synthetic polymer paint; each 20 x 16 in.**

Turquoise Marilyn, **1964. Acrylic and silk-screen ink on canvas. 40 x 40 in.**
Private collection. © 2004 Andy Warhol Foundation
for the Visual Arts/Artists Rights Society (ARS), New York.

129 Die in Jet (Plane Crash), 1962. Synthetic polymer paint on canvas. 100 x 72 in.
© The Andy Warhol Foundation, Inc./Art Resource, NY. © 2004 Andy Warhol Foundation
for the Visual Art/Artists Rights Society (ARS), New York.

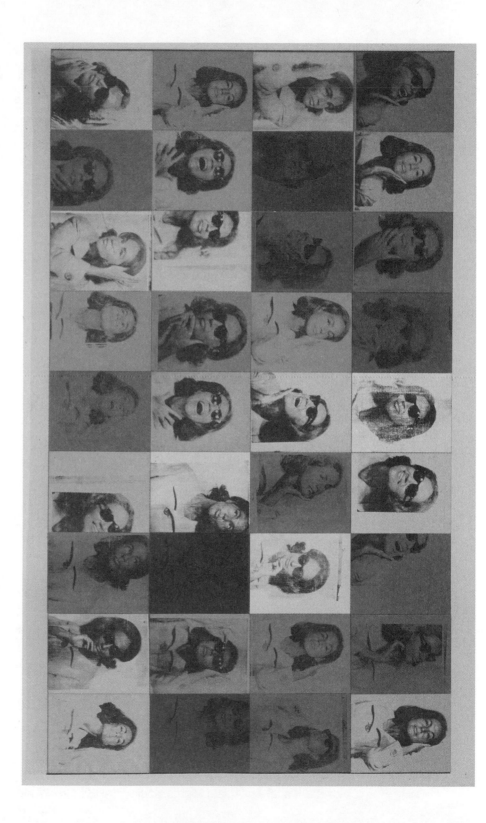

Ethel Scull 36 Times, 1963. Synthetic polymer paint silk-screened on canvas; each panel 19-7/8 x 15-7/8 in.; total dimensions 79-3/4 x 143-1/4 in. Whitney Museum of American Art, New York. Jointly owned by the Whitney Museum of American Art and the Metropolitan Museum of Art. Gift of Ethel Redner Scull.

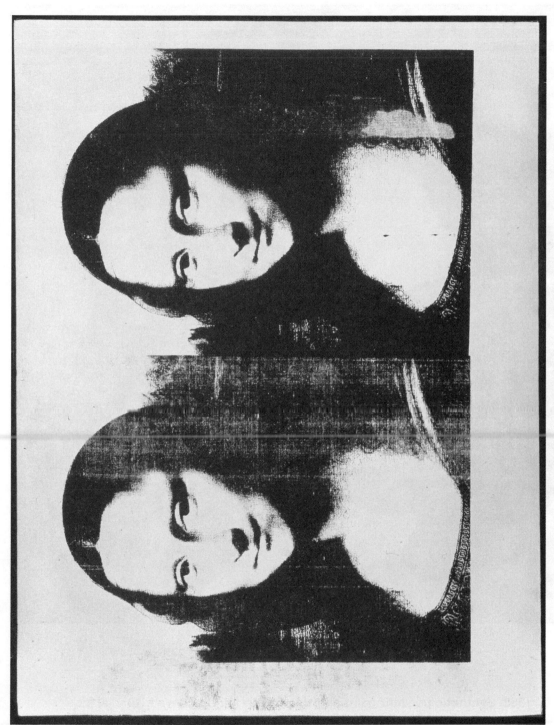

Double Mona Lisa, 1963. Silk-screen ink on canvas. 38-1/2 x 37-1/8 in.

© The Andy Warhol Foundation, Inc./Art Resource, NY. © 2004 Andy Warhol Foundation for the Visual Arts/Artists Rights Society (ARS), New York.

Liz, **1963. Synthetic polymer paint and silk-screen ink on canvas. 40 x 40 in.**

Race Riot a Pair, **1964. Silk-screen ink on canvas. Each 30 x 33 in.**
Private collection. © 2004 Andy Warhol Foundation
for the Visual Arts/Artists Rights Society (ARS), New York.

Electric Chair, 1963. Synthetic polymer paint and silk-screen ink on canvas. 20 x 30 in.

***Elvis I & II*, 1964. Two panels: synthetic polymer paint and silk-screen ink on canvas; aluminum paint and silk-screen ink on canvas; each 82 x 82 in.**

Elvis and Elvis Presley are registered trademarks of Elvis Presley Enterprises, Inc. © The Andy Warhol Foundation, Inc./Art Resource, NY. © 2004 Andy Warhol Foundation for the Visual Arts/Artists Rights Society (ARS), New York.

16 Jackies, **1964. Sixteen panels: synthetic polymer paint and silk-screen ink**
on canvas; each 20 x 16 in.; total dimensions 80 x 64 in.
© The Andy Warhol Foundation, Inc./Art Resource, NY. © Andy Warhol Foundation
for the Visual Arts/Artists Rights Society (ARS), New York.

Andy at work on large Flower painting, the Factory, New York City, March 1965.
Photograph by David McCabe.

Flowers, **1971. Silk screen. 36 x 36 in.**
Private collection. © 2004 Andy Warhol Foundation for the Visual Arts/Artists Rights Society (ARS), New York.

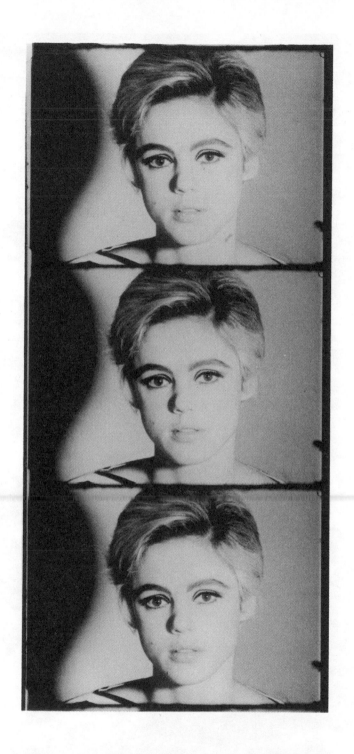

Screen Test: Edie Sedgwick, **1965. 16mm film.**

Factory regulars at 33 Union Square, 1968. Bottom row, left to right: Ingrid Superstar, Ondine, Tom Baker, Tiger Morse, Billy Name, Andy Warhol. Top row, left to right: Nico, Brigid Polk (aka Brigid Berlin), Louis Waldon, Taylor Mead, Ultra Violet, Paul Morrissey, Viva, International Velvet, unidentified person.

Gerard Malanga Collection.

Late Self-Portrait, **1967. Silk-screen ink on canvas. 22 x 22 in.**
Private collection. © 2004 Andy Warhol Foundation
for the Visual Arts/Artists Rights Society (ARS), New York.

everything beautiful under the sun

Interview

june 1993

Madonna's dressed!
in photos by Herb Ritts
butt Lenny's not!
Plus fathers and sons bare their souls
& a clear view of fashion's future

$2.95 USA $3.50 CAN £1.75 UK

Interview **magazine, June 1993.**
Photograph by Herb Ritts. Courtesy Brant Publications, Inc.

Muhammad Ali, **1977. Synthetic polymer paint and silk-screen ink on canvas. 40 x 40 in.**
© The Andy Warhol Foundation, Inc./Art Resource, NY. © 2004 Andy Warhol Foundation
for the Visual Arts/Artists Rights Society (ARS), New York.

Mao, **1973. Acrylic and screen on canvas. 50 x 42 in.**
Private collection. © 2004 Andy Warhol Foundation
for the Visual Arts/Artists Rights Society (ARS), New York.

Vote McGovern, **1972. Screen print on Arches paper. 42 x 42 in.**
© The Andy Warhol Foundation, Inc./Art Resource, NY. © 2004 Andy Warhol Foundation
for the Visual Arts/Artists Rights Society (ARS), New York.

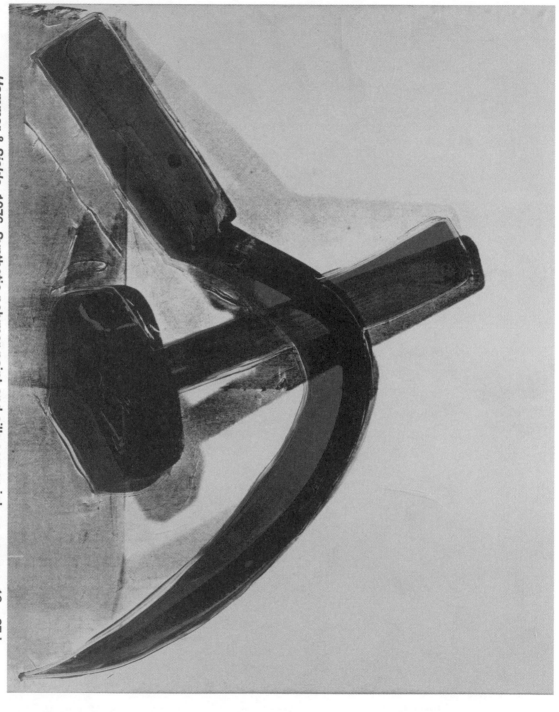

Hammer & Sickle, 1976. Synthetic polymer paint and silk-screen ink on canvas. 18 x 27 in.
© The Andy Warhol Foundation, Inc./Art Resource, NY. © 2004 Andy Warhol Foundation
for the Visual Arts/Artists Rights Society (ARS), New York.

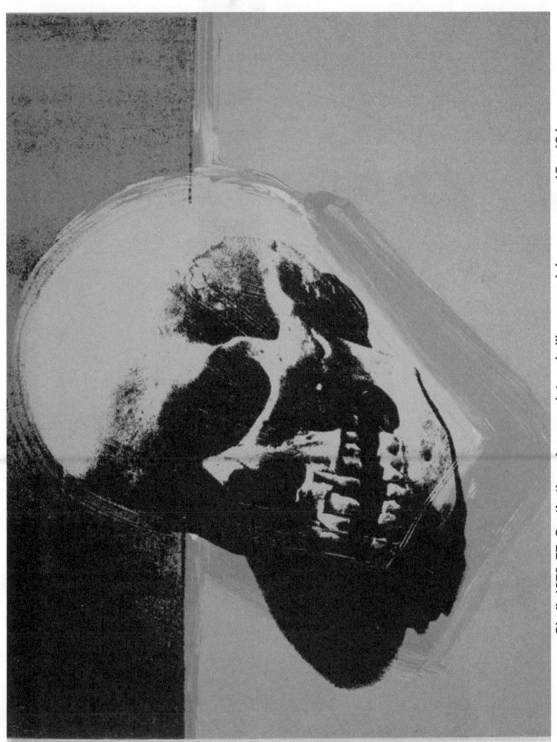

Skull, 1976–77. Synthetic polymer paint and silk-screen ink on canvas. 15 x 19 in.
© The Andy Warhol Foundation, Inc./Art Resource, NY. © 2004 Andy Warhol Foundation for the Visual Arts/Artists Rights Society (ARS), New York.

Shadows, 1978–79. Installation of 72 of 102 paintings. Acrylic, variously silk-screened and painted canvas; each 76 x 52 in. Installation view at Dia:Beacon, Dia Art Foundation, Beacon, New York.

**Exhibition poster for the Andy Warhol/Jean-Michel Basquiat
show at the Tony Shafrazi Gallery, New York, 1985.**

Campbell's Soup, **1985. Acrylic on canvas. 73 x 60 in.**

$9, 1982. Screen print on Lenox museum board. 40 x 32 in.

Last Supper **(yellow), 1986. Synthetic polymer paint and**
silk-screen ink on canvas. 40 x 40 in.
Private collection. © 2004 Andy Warhol Foundation
for the Visual Arts/Artists Rights Society (ARS), New York.

followed by a series of other films, including *L'Amour, Frankenstein,* and *Dracula* in 3-D. Then in 1978, after a flop entitled *Bad,* about a gang of female hoodlums, Andy stopped making movies altogether. Jed Johnson directed this last film, and its failure caused the beginning of a rift in their relationship.

Four years earlier, though, Andy had bought a new town house, and Jed and their dachshunds, Archie and Amos, moved in with him. Jed decorated the place with the soon-to-be-fashionable early-nineteenth-century Empire furniture and stashed away some of the more eccentric stuff that Andy compulsively collected.

By now, thanks to Fred Hughes, who liked to mix with English aristocrats, and Paul Morrissey, who disapproved of drugs, the Factory had cleaned up its act. It had moved to another building in Union Square and was set up like a regular office. The silver foil and strobe lights were retired; the rock-and-roll sixties were a bygone era. Brigid joined Alcoholics Anonymous and stopped drinking, though she still sat at the front desk when she and Andy weren't having one of their spats.

Several times a week Fred hosted luncheons to entertain clients, celebrities, and advertisers. In the new upmarket studio style, a French Art Deco table and chairs from Andy's collection of antiques graced the dining room. He would sit speechless during these lunches of carry-out pasta salad or pâté, while Bob Colacello or Fred and some of the young "talkers" kept the conversation going. Afterward Andy would disappear into his studio, where photo sessions and portrait production took place.

Gone were the black leather jacket and motorcycle boots. Now Andy sported a designer jacket and tie. He still wore jeans, a holdover from the sixties, and this look caught on in the fashion magazines. Andy would gripe to Brigid that the good old days were over. In truth the shooting had made him apprehensive about going anywhere unescorted. Most of Andy's socializing for the next few years took place at private parties or at discos such as Studio 54, where Andy stopped by almost every night when he was in town. It was all about business at the Factory. But Andy, the consummate artist, still had other ideas up his sleeve.

Andy Warhol Enterprises 1975–1982

Buying is much more American than thinking, and I'm as American as they come. —Andy Warhol

Silver-wigged, Andy sat in the window of the Famous-Barr department store in downtown St. Louis. With Velvet Underground music blasting into the street, Andy autographed copies of his new book, *The Philosophy of Andy Warhol: From A to B and Back Again*. Inside a red-and-white cover reminiscent of a soup can, the book offered frank, funny, gossipy takes on Andy's life in the fast lane of New York. A couple of Andy's aphorisms were "People should fall in love with their eyes closed. Just close your eyes. And don't look" and "Money is the moment to me. Money is my mood."

Bemused passersby packed the store to purchase the book. That night at a party, Andy stood in a corner and signed real Campbell's soup cans, cocktail napkins, and anything else guests waved in front of him. St. Louis was just one of the stops Fred Hughes had arranged in his nationwide promotional tour. His ulterior motive was to drum up portrait commissions.

After his profitable book tour, Andy returned to New York, where he continued to fill Time Capsules with the debris of his life. In 1974 he had come up with this solution to his aversion to throwing anything out. Now, instead of helter-skelter piles that drove his staff crazy, he kept a tidy carton, designated a Time Capsule, sitting by his desk. As he opened the mail, checks and party invitations were saved. Everything else he dropped into his Time Capsules: press releases, movie magazines, worn-out batteries from his tape recorder, art catalogs, fan letters, test reels for films, sketches, old shoes. (One recently opened Time Capsule contained a mummified human foot.) He dated the cartons, saying they would be valuable someday and could be auctioned off. In twelve years he filled about six hundred cartons, which are now being opened and cataloged one by one at the Andy Warhol Museum in Pittsburgh.

In 1977 Andy painted one of his most political series, the Hammer & Sickle still lifes. This potent image of Communism symbolized the solidarity between the farmers and factory workers of the Soviet Union. Scouting for pictures of the tools, his assistant, Ronnie Cutrone, returned with a hammer and sickle from the hardware store and photographed them in various combinations. Andy chose the colors that pleased him. The paintings achieve a strong graphic effect with harsh contrasting colors, such as black and red with orange shadows on a white ground. The Hammer & Sickle Series differed sharply from the society portraits Andy had been turning out. Yet he disavowed any overt political intention, saying that he had been inspired by the Communist symbols he had noticed graffitied on walls all over Rome.

This series was followed by a set of macabre skull paintings, drawings and collages made from a photograph of an antique skull Andy brought back from Paris. He requested that Ronnie Cutrone make some side-lit photographs of the skull that included long shadows. In the photograph he chose for the painting, the shadow looks like a profile of a baby.

Andy's absorption with shadows culminated in a series in which shadows themselves were the subject. He made 103 Shadow paintings, mysterious abstract pieces that he envisioned hung in one vast room to form an art "environment." He called it "disco décor" and joked that the paintings would be critically dismissed but that the party would get rave reviews. At the dinner after the opening, however, when a reviewer called his work decorative, Andy blew up. The next day he told his diarist, Pat Hackett, "That got me really mad, and I'm so embarrassed everybody saw the real me. I got so red and was telling him off." Andy was usually so skilled at "putting his Andy on" that sometimes people forgot the serious artist hidden behind the pose.

There are several different stories about how the Shadow paintings were made. Ronnie Cutrone said that Andy always loved the way his paintings looked at the corners, where the silk screen faded into a scattering of dots. He'd say, "Oh, that looks so pretty! What can we do that's abstract?"

So Ronnie built various small models out of cardboard. They were placed in a strong light and only their shadows photographed. Others say that the Shadows were taken from Polaroids that Andy shot for a later series of male and female nudes he called Torsos. Whatever their source, the paintings themselves have an otherworldly presence. Andy's work almost always had an underlying preoccupation with death. Even though he had recovered from the shooting and enjoyed a luxurious and interesting lifestyle, the prospect of death lay not far beneath the surface. "I don't want to live forever. Do you?" he asked friends out of the blue one night at dinner.

The Last Years   1982–1987

I go to the small Roman Catholic church round the corner from my house most Sundays. I haven't been to confession for some while. I've nothing to confess. —Andy Warhol

Jean-Michel Basquiat worshipped Andy Warhol. Of Haitian and Puerto Rican descent, the twenty-three-year-old artist came from a middle-class family. As a teenager, Jean-Michel achieved notoriety in New York by painting graffiti, signed SAMO, on subway walls and choosing to sleep on the streets. Just as Andy had once bombarded Truman Capote with letters and drawings, Basquiat sent his hero notes and showed up unannounced at the Factory, where he was turned away. Under the new, careful rules, those without introductions weren't welcome. Finally, through Andy's Swiss dealer, Bruno Bischofberger, Jean-Michel was invited for lunch. A number of articles had appeared in art magazines about the artist's graffiti-inspired paintings, and Andy, always on the lookout for new talent, had agreed to trade portraits with him. At lunch Jean-Michel charmed Andy, who had a Polaroid taken of them together. A few hours later the young artist reappeared at the Factory with a portrait, still wet, he'd painted of the two of them.

From then on, entries in Andy's diary refer to Jean-Michel—their trip to Milan, workouts with a trainer, and parties attended together. Both women and men were attracted to the striking young man with untamed dreadlocks and an even more untamed nature. Ambitious and talented, Basquiat lived recklessly, staying up all night, taking drugs, and going from one girlfriend to another. (Madonna dated him just before both their careers took off.) Andy adopted a protective attitude toward the younger artist, arranging for him to move out of his squalid digs into a downtown loft that Andy owned.

When they started painting together, Andy was amazed by Jean-Michel's energy. The collaborative process always stimulated his own creativity. With Jean-Michel at his side, he found himself painting for hours. It made him feel young. He put away his coat and tie and donned a black leather jacket again to emulate the hip young artist. Andy contributed to their duo canvases by hand-painting corporate logos and newspaper headlines, while Jean-Michel added his primitive line drawings and macabre figures.

The new group of hot young artists on the New York art scene regarded Andy as their greatest influence. This group encompassed Kenny Scharf and Keith Haring, who like Basquiat made graffiti paintings, as well as the more expressionistic artists such as Julian Schnabel, who used realistic subject matter—cartoons, ordinary objects, references to art history, or personal images. They also aggressively promoted themselves, relishing publicity and flaunting their respective lifestyles. All this was part of the Pop Art legacy. And as the eighties were a time of economic growth in America, many newly rich tycoons spent money as fast as they could make it. In turn, critics, collectors, and museum curators clamored to discover the next new flavor in art. To many, art was simply another commodity, driven by greed and celebrity.

Ironically, Andy's art had captured this era of excess since the sixties, exposing all its pretensions. From the ordinary soup can of his early career to the dazzling portraits of celebrities, he had documented his own rise. Characteristically deadpan, Andy said, "Business art is the step that comes after Art. . . . making money is art and working is art and good business the best art." Perhaps it was natural for the new generation of artists to emulate the Warhol style. Enjoying instant fame and instant wealth, they lived like rock stars. Most of them would experience a downfall in the nineties. But during this period, the business of art was booming.

After a few years, however, the relationship between Andy and his "art mascot," as one journalist called Basquiat, was on the verge of disintegrating. Andy's relentless appearances at every party and disco belied a prudent life. He still avoided drugs, drank little, and ate moderately. No matter how wild the lives around him became, Andy did his work. Jean-Michel, on the other hand, lived self-destructively. His paintings fetched high prices, but he squandered his commissions on more dangerous drugs and drank too much at dinners, either falling asleep at the table or getting into brawls. Andy's close friend and the advertising director of *Interview*, Paige Powell, was involved in a love affair with Jean-Michel, who would disappear for days, causing her continuous stress. Worried, Andy, who usually ignored friends' self-destructive behavior, lectured him to no avail. The last straw came with their joint exhibit at the Tony Shafrazi Gallery. The reviews, as well as sales, were so poor that Jean-Michel turned against his mentor and went his own disastrous way. By the time he was twenty-seven, he would be dead of a drug overdose. But his paintings, now in many museums, influenced a number of artists of the next generation, who imitated his compelling, naive, primitive style.

Andy now decided to exhibit a group of bad-boy Oxidation paintings from 1978, described tactfully by the Gagosian Gallery as composed of mixed media on copper metallic paint on canvas. Critic Ingrid Sischy, writing in the *New York Times* in 2003, put it more bluntly: "What could be more wicked than the oxidation paintings? These works—the result of Warhol's getting some of the Factory crowd to urinate on prepared canvases, which then oxidized over time— had the maestro squealing with laughter at the time they were done, and it is hard to look at them today without a private giggle."

Andy also threw himself into physical workouts to rebuild his strength. In spite of his continuing insecurity about his looks, he had signed up with a modeling agency, which booked him for fashion shoots and magazines, posing him with models and other celebrities. People said he was making a fool of himself, but Andy didn't care. He loved being famous, and every advertisement, endorsement, and appearance was another confirmation that the poor Ruthenian boy from Pittsburgh had made it.

Despite all the media exposure, people close to Andy talked about how lonely he was. Pat Hackett said, "He lost steam in the last few years. . . . He was always afraid of getting sick or going broke. He needed something to lift his spirits." She also commented that Andy was no longer the mischief maker who had stirred up trouble among the denizens of the old Factory. Now she said he was tired of drama—"He was kinder and easier to be around than at any time since I'd met him."

All his life, shopping had cheered him up. Although Andy was not the type to reflect on the past, he loved nostalgic artifacts. Every day he made his way from his uptown house down to the studio, stopping at antique stores, auction houses, and flea markets. His friend Stuart Pivar picked Andy up in his limousine, loading it with objects from old silver and jewelry to cookie jars. Dressed in a black turtleneck and jeans, holding copies of *Interview* to give out to fans who approached him on the street, Andy would ask shopkeepers in his deadpan voice, "Do you have any masterpieces?"

By now Jed Johnson had left Andy and gone out on his own to open an interior design business, only stopping back on the weekends to pick up the dogs, Amos and Archie, whose custody they shared. Friends thought Andy was brokenhearted, but he refused to discuss it. Without Jed's restraining influence, closets in Andy's town house spilled over with collectibles—Fiestaware, Mickey Mouse and Popeye figures, Native American artifacts, Art Deco furniture, old watches, weather vanes, whirligigs, tin boxes with faded coffee or tea logos, paintings, bronze statuary, and more. Unopened boxes and bags piled up everywhere, but Andy didn't show his treasure trove to anyone. Close friends who stopped by to pick him up before an event were expected to wait on the sidewalk in front of the house. Perhaps he thought if his employees saw how rich he was, they would not put up with such low salaries. And worse, clients might object to the high prices he charged for portraits. He had always separated the private Andy from the public Andy.

Many of his paintings now were commissioned to glorify products, including the Campbell Soup Company. Hoping to regain their diminishing market, the executives were delighted with his paintings of their new soup boxes, executed in a painterly style with the label spread flat across the canvas. Andy also produced drawings and paintings of Mercedes-Benz racing cars. There also were new series based on various themes: Cowboys and Indians, Paintings for Children, Animals: Species at Risk, and Dollar Signs. Meanwhile, his early paintings, including a dollar-bill canvas from Bob and Ethel Scull's collection, fetched high prices at auction.

His last series of Self-Portraits (see book jacket) were silk screens of a frightening headshot, his hair standing on end, his face resembling a death mask. Some of the heads, against a black background, appeared in Day-Glo purple, pink, and green. Others were painted in multicolored camouflage patterns taken from a swatch purchased at an army-navy store. Andy's unspoken guarantee to clients was that their portrait would be flattering, but he made no such promise to himself. In the tradition of other great portrait artists, he recorded his own image over time with unflinching candor. Agonized, ghostlike, the face that leaps out at us reveals the private Andy, the seer who saw too much. "I paint pictures of myself to remind myself that I'm still around," Andy said. When these Self-Portraits were exhibited, friends were deeply moved by what they perceived as Andy's view of his approaching end. And Andy himself, in his wig, with his pale face and sunken cheeks, his skin tightened by collagen injections, looked very different from the offbeat, shy young man who had first come to New York thirty years before.

Passages in the diary he dictated on the phone each

morning to Pat Hackett indicated how unsatisfied he felt by the life he led. He told friends he longed to do something more meaningful. Paige Powell brought him with her to work in a church soup kitchen. Always dejected on holidays, he spent Christmas and Easter helping out at the shelter, dishing out turkey and pie to the homeless. He liked the fact that no one there had any idea who he was.

Many of his old friends had died of AIDS, drugs, or suicide. Bob Colacello had quit *Interview* to focus on his own projects. Fred Hughes, tired of Andy's demands, all but ignored him. Andy still had loyal Pat Hackett at the other end of the telephone every morning, recording his diary of gossip and expenses, and Brigid Berlin to make him laugh. And there was always a party with famous people to go to. But Andy's diary entries reflect a sad wistfulness. Andy Warhol, at fifty-nine, was feeling old. Although he depended on visits to skin doctors, nutritionists, trainers, crystal healers, and physical therapists, he refused to visit his regular physician, suspicious of modern medicine. The most positive side of Andy's life remained his work.

Andy based his last great series on *The Last Supper,* a famous painting by the Renaissance artist Leonardo da Vinci. He planned the series to be exhibited at a gallery in Milan, where tourists flocked to see the original. Instead of working from a good reproduction (the original was badly decomposed anyway), he chose to silk-screen from cheap secondary sources, including a plaster mock-up he found in Times Square. On some of the Last Suppers, he dripped paint from a brush onto the surface. There were a number of versions, from silk screens to hand-painted ones, using camouflage grounds, overlapping grids, and multiple color combinations. The most spectacular canvases were 10' by 20'. Despite being immediately recognizable as copies, they have a power and beauty all their own. "If visitors can't get in to see the original *Last Supper,*" said Andy, "they can cross the street and see mine." That was the kind of flip remark that Andy's public expected. Few people realized how frequently Andy attended mass at the Catholic church around the corner from his house or understood that the religious paintings might be more to him than just another cultural icon.

In America, where art lovers had always sought the next new thing, Andy's work no longer shocked. Pop was old hat. But in Europe he was a god, besieged by fans from Italy to Germany and France. Thousands of Milanese gathered for the opening of his Last Supper exhibit amid flashing cameras and reporters. "I think an artist is anybody who does something well, like if you cook well," he told an interviewer. During the excitement surrounding the opening, Andy experienced pains in his stomach and went back to the hotel early.

On his return to New York, doctors diagnosed a gallbladder problem and advised him to have it removed immediately. Andy was frightened of the operation and put it off. After a few weeks, under pressure from friends, he made an appointment to be admitted to New York Hospital. "I'm not going to make it," he repeated over and over. "I'm not coming out of the hospital." His assistant Ken Leland checked him in under an assumed name. "Are any famous people here?" Andy asked. "You're the only one," came the reply. When Andy was settled in his bed, he started to shiver. Ken put his leather jacket around Andy and turned on the TV. When he left, Ken said later, Andy seemed in better spirits.

Whether there was negligence on the part of the private nurse or carelessness by the hospital, which did not carefully check his medical records, no one is certain. But on Sunday,

February 22, at 6:31 in the morning, after a routine gall-bladder operation, Andy Warhol was pronounced dead of complications relating to the surgery.

"Pop Art's King Dies!" announced the headline in the *New York Post*. "Posterity may well decide that his times deserved him and were lucky to have got him," wrote John Russell in the *New York Times.*

Postscript

When I die I don't want to leave any leftovers. I'd like to disappear. People wouldn't say he died today, they'd say he disappeared. But I do like the idea of people turning into dust or sand, and it would be very glamorous to be reincarnated as a big ring on Elizabeth Taylor's finger. —Andy Warhol (read by Nicholas Love at Andy's memorial mass in 1987)

134

On a cold gray day in late February 1987, a small band of mourners huddled together on a hillside cemetery in a lower-class suburb of Pittsburgh to say farewell to Andy Warhol. The priest shook holy water over the casket, and Paige Powell pitched a copy of *Interview* and a bottle of Beautiful, Andy's favorite perfume, into the grave. Andy was buried next to his mother and father. Leo Castelli and a few luminaries sent orchids, but with the exception of Fred Hughes, Andy's lawyer, Ed Hayes, and a few staff people from the Factory, the cast of characters that had comprised Andy's illustrious New York world stayed home. Although Andy's brothers, John and Paul, preferred a private service, they resented the fact that not only had Fred interfered with the details of Andy's funeral, but he also had taken over control of their brother's estate. Friends from Pittsburgh who attended expressed disappointment over the lack of celebrities at the burial of their hometown hero.

In New York two months later, a grand memorial service, orchestrated by Fred, took place on April Fools' Day. St. Patrick's Cathedral overflowed with bouquets of white tulips, Andy's favorite flower. The organ droned solemnly as two thousand people from all periods in Andy's life streamed in to pay their respects to the Prince of Pop. Andy's brothers and their families flew in from Pittsburgh. Liza Minnelli, Jean-Michel Basquiat, and Baby Jane Holzer were there. Gerard Malanga turned up in a white T-shirt that read DEAD AT 58. A conservatively dressed Brigid Berlin, barely recognizable to old Factory friends, read a passage from the Bible. Yoko Ono spoke about how kind Andy had been to her son after John Lennon's death, offering to do a portrait of him every year on his birthday.

The great art critic John Richardson gave a moving eulogy. Mentioning Andy's lifelong practice of attending mass regularly, he said, "Never take Andy at face value. The callous observer was, in fact, a recording angel. And Andy's detachment, the distance he established between the world and himself, was, above all, a matter of innocence and of art." Andy Warhol belonged to a long tradition of artists and writers whose charge it was to gain a new perspective on things by standing back and bearing witness. Posterity judges an artist's greatness, but certainly while Andy lived, his work, with all its detractors, had been taken seriously. He had profoundly influenced both high art and popular culture. Advertising, especially on TV, took its cue from Andy's Pop Art style with its Day-Glo colors, repetition, common objects, and laid-back wit. Young painters and video artists emulated his style and, in the case of the top few, took it a step further.

During those weeks before the service, however, the wheels of commerce continued to turn. A flurry of activity took place at the Factory as Andy's assistants put the finishing touches on artworks. Paintings were crated and shipped out to various places, including to a warehouse for storage. A curtain of secrecy, penetrated only by Fred Hughes and Ed Hayes, seemed to cover these activities. At Andy's town house the appraisers for the estate entered to find a mind-boggling clutter of treasures and junk, from Navajo rugs to Art Deco pottery. The man who once said people were burdened by too many objects had amassed more than ten thousand items, including fine furniture, jewelry and artworks. Andy's will stipulated that the proceeds from the sale of his art and belongings be used to set up a foundation to support grants for artists, arts organizations, and art-related projects.

A year later, at Sotheby's auction house in New York, the bulk of Andy's possessions sold for $25.3 million, well over the estimate. His cookie jar collection went for a mind-boggling $250,000. By then the name Andy Warhol possessed enough star power to attract six thousand people, who waited for hours to see all that he had amassed. Not long after the auction, a crate holding a cache of gems and watches was found hidden in a secret drawer in a storeroom of the town house. This brought another million and a half. Some thought a few of Andy's things had disappeared, but no one could prove it. And, of course, his stocks and bonds, licensing agreements, artworks, films, and book projects had even greater value. The wiggy artist from Pittsburgh was worth a fortune, more than anyone had dreamed, and his estate would be put to good use. The Andy Warhol Museum in

Pittsburgh and the Andy Warhol Foundation continue his legacy today.

Andy's retrospective exhibition at the Museum of Modern Art in 1989, spanning three decades of his astounding, prolific career, secured his place in art history. From his whimsical shoe drawings to his early Pop paintings, from his silkscreen portraits of celebrities to his poignant and disturbing Disaster Series, from his Self-Portraits to his enormous *Last Supper* painting, three floors of the museum documented his development as an artist who spoke to the American public about its greatest desires and fears.

In 2002, at the opening of the Andy Warhol retrospective at the Los Angeles Museum of Contemporary Art, he was proclaimed one of the greatest and most influential artists of the twentieth century. Crowds lined up before an archway of giant Brillo boxes leading into a party that would have made Andy proud. The evening celebrated not only his art but the man himself, now a larger-than-life American icon, a world-famous cult figure. Andy's pale face and silver wig, along with his paintings of Campbell's soup cans and Marilyn Monroe, were recognized everywhere. Leading up to the exhibit, drag queens costumed as some of the more outrageous Superstars who graced his films greeted the guests. A rock band played songs from the sixties. Inside the museum, Andy's work, spanning a career rivaling Picasso's in terms of production, filled the walls—blazing with Day-Glo color, spellbinding, amusing, and fresh as ever to the dazzled crowd.

The shy boy who once dreamed of being a serious artist had become a legend in his own time—far surpassing the fifteen minutes of fame he had predicted for everyone else. Today Andy's influence continues to be felt not only in the art world but also in the world of advertising and fashion. Lisa

Philips, the director of the New Museum, said, "Since Andy Warhol, expectations about the artist and the marketplace have changed rapidly. In a post-Warholian world, all of it flies." The myth of Andy Warhol has endured, and although his paintings look as timely as the day he made them, they also provide a picture of the last half of a century in which Pop reigned and the rags-to-riches American dream was expertly played out in Warhol's world.

some important dates

1928

On August 6 Andrew Warhola is born in Pittsburgh, Pennsylvania, to Andrej and Julia Zavacky Warhola.

1934–36

Andy attends Holmes Elementary through eighth grade. He skips several grades.

1936–37

Andy has rheumatic fever, which leads to a "nervous break-down" (St. Vitus' dance). He spends two months in bed, coloring, cutting, and playing with paper dolls.

1937–41

Andy attends a free art program at the Carnegie Institute, part of the Pittsburgh Art Museum complex.

1942

Andy's father dies after a three-year illness.

1945

Andy graduates from Schenley High School in Pittsburgh.

1945–49

Andy attends Carnegie Institute of Technology (now Carnegie Mellon University) in Pittsburgh.

Andy is picture editor of the college art magazine. His painting

The Broad Gave Me My Face but I Can Pick My Own Nose is included in an alternative exhibit.

Andy graduates with a BFA, moves to New York City, and shares an apartment with fellow student and artist Philip Pearlstein. Andy begins drawing advertisements for various magazines, including *Glamour, Vogue,* and *Harper's Bazaar,* and for companies such as I. Miller and Tiffany.

1950

Andy moves into an apartment on East 75th Street and his mother, Julia, moves in with him. He buys his first television.

1952

Andy has his first solo exhibit at the Hugo Gallery in New York, a series of drawings inspired by Truman Capote's stories.

1953–55

Andy joins a theater group and designs sets. Serendipity, a store on the Upper East Side, sells his drawings and books, including *25 Cats Name Sam and One Blue Pussy.* He moves with his mother to a duplex on Lexington Avenue. Later he moves to a house on East 87th Street.

1956

Andy takes a trip around the world with Charles Lisanby, a television set designer. One of Andy's shoe drawings is included in his first group show at the Museum of Modern Art in New York. He receives the thirty-sixth Annual Art Director's Award of Distinctive Merit for his I. Miller and hat designs.

1959

Andy publishes *Wild Raspberries,* a cookbook, with Susie Frankfurt.

1960

Andy and his mother move to 1342 Lexington Avenue. Andy makes his first hand-painted pictures of comic strips, including Dick Tracy, Popeye, and Superman, and paints two of his Coca-Cola bottles.

1961

Andy's comic strip paintings are used in window displays at the Bonwit Teller department store. He buys the lightbulb drawing from Ivan Karp at the Leo Castelli Gallery. Karp visits his studio.

1962

Andy paints dollar bills and Campbell's soup cans and has a show of the soup cans at the Ferus Gallery in Los Angeles. He makes his first silk screens in May and the Marllyns In October and is included in a group show at the Sidney Janis Gallery in New York. In November, Eleanor Ward shows his work at the Stable Gallery. He gives up his commerical work, which had financed his artistic work.

1963

Andy rents a studio in a firehouse. He meets Gerard Malanga, who becomes his assistant. In the fall he drives to Los Angeles for a show at the Ferus Gallery. He makes his films *Sleep* in New York and *Tarzan and Jane Regained . . . Sort of* in Los Angeles. In November President John F.

Kennedy is assassinated in Dallas, and the following month Andy makes *Red Jackie,* the first in his Jackie Series.

1964
At the end of 1963 or beginning of 1964, Andy moves to a loft at 231 East 47th Street, the first Factory. A watershed year for his skyrocketing career. In January he shows the Disaster pictures at his first solo exhibit in Europe at Galerie Ileana Sonnabend in Paris. The architect Philip Johnson commissions Andy to make a mural for the New York State Pavilion in New York at the World's Fair. It is painted over for political reasons. Andy wins the Independent Film Award from *Film Culture* magazine. Four of his films are shown at the New York Film Festival at Lincoln Center. His first solo show takes place at the Leo Castelli Gallery. He makes his Brillo Boxes and other sculpture, as well as his first Self-Portrait Series.

1965
Andy goes back to Paris for the Flowers exhibit at Sonnabend, along with Edie Sedgewick and Gerard Malanga, and visits Tangiers. In Paris, Andy announces he will not continue to paint but will concentrate on making films. That summer, he meets Paul Morrissey. Andy's first solo museum exhibition takes place at the Institute of Contemporary Art at the University of Pennsylvania. In December, he meets the rock group the Velvet Underground.

1966
The film *Chelsea Girls* is made and becomes the first underground film to be shown at a commercial theater in New

York. The Velvet Underground and German singer Nico perform at the Dom, a dance hall on St. Mark's Place. Leo Castelli exhibits the Cow Wallpaper and the Silver Clouds.

1967

Andy visits San Francisco for a screening of *Chelsea Girls* and attends the Cannes Film Festival. Six Self-Portraits are shown at the United States Pavilion in Canada at Expo '67. He goes on tour to speak at college campuses, and hires Alan Midgette to impersonate him at his lectures. Andy meets Fred Hughes, who later becomes president of Andy Warhol Enterprises.

1968

Andy moves the Factory to 33 Union Square. He meets Jed Johnson. Andy has his first solo museum exhibition at the Modern Museum in Stockholm. He is shot by Valerie Solanas, founder and sole member of SCUM, the Society for Cutting Up Men. He spends two months in the hospital. He creates *Clouds*, the set for a Merce Cunningham ballet.

1969

The film *Trash* is made. In the fall, the first issue of *Inter/VIEW* magazine is published. (Spelling later changed.)

1970

Andy curates a show for the Rhode Island School of Design titled "Raid the Icebox I with Andy Warhol." Throughout the 1970s, Andy creates endorsements for various companies, including Air France, Puerto Rican Rum, and *U.S. News & World Report*.

1971

Andy's play *Pork* opens in London. He has a number of exhibitions in Europe.

1972

Andy begins painting officially again (although he has never completely stopped). He primarily paints portraits of stars and society types. Julia Warhola dies at the age of eighty in Pittsburgh.

1974–75

Andy moves the Factory to 860 Broadway, where it develops more of an office atmosphere.

He moves his residence, with Jed Johnson, to a town house at 57 East 66th Street, where he lives until his death. A major retrospective of his work is mounted at the Kunsthaus in Zurich. Andy publishes *The Philosophy of Andy Warhol*. He tours the country and has exhibitions at the Greenberg Gallery in St. Louis, Margo Leavin in Los Angeles, and other galleries.

1976–77

Andy does the Skull Series and the Hammer & Sickle Series. The Museum of American Folk Art in New York shows his folk art collection. Studio 54 opens in April 1977.

1979–80

The Whitney Museum of American Art mounts an exhibition of Andy's portraits titled "Portraits of the 70s." He makes the Reversals, Retrospectives, and Shadow Series.

1980

From 1980 until he dies in 1987, Andy travels to openings of his shows in the United States and Europe. He incorporates diamond powder in a series called Diamond Dust Shoes. He produces a show on cable television called *Andy Warhol's TV*. His book with Pat Hackett, *POPism: The Warhol Sixties,* is published.

1981

Andy does the series Myth, Dollar Signs, Crosses, Gun, and Knives. His work is exhibited in galleries and museums from Tokyo to Los Angeles.

1982

Andy exhibits at Documenta in Kasel, Germany. He visits Berlin, Paris, Zurich, and cities in China. *Andy Warhol Television* is shown on cable TV.

1983

Andy makes the Animals: Species at Risk Series.

1984–85

Andy makes the Ads Series. He collaborates on paintings with Jean-Michel Basquiat. Andy's book of photographs, *America,* is published.

1987

Andy Warhol dies of complications after a routine gallbladder operation. He is buried in Pittsburgh. A memorial service, organized by Fred Hughes, is later held in New York City.

1988

Andy's collection of antiques, jewelry, art objects, and crafts brings record-breaking prices at two auctions. The proceeds go to the Andy Warhol Foundation, set up to promote the visual arts.

1989

"Andy Warhol: A Retrospective" is held at the Museum of Modern Art in New York.

1994

The Andy Warhol Museum opens in Pittsburgh. In the following years, many exhibitions of Andy's paintings are mounted in Europe, Japan, and the United States.

2001

An Andy Warhol retrospective opens at the Museum of Contemporary Art, Los Angeles, after a stint at the Neue Nationalgalerie, Berlin, and at the Tate Modern, London.

2003

Several of Andy's films are given a retrospective at BAM (the Brooklyn Academy of Music) in New York.

selected films by andy warhol

Sleep July 1963

Tarzan and Jane Regained . . . Sort of October 1963

Kiss November–December 1963

Haircut End of 1963

Screen Tests 1964–66

Empire July 25–26, 1964

Henry Geldzahler July 25–26, 1964

Harlot December 1964 (first sound film)

13 Most Beautiful Girls 1964

13 Most Beautiful Boys 1964

The Life of Juanita Castro January 1965

Horse January 1965

Vinyl March 1965

Poor Little Rich Girl March–April 1965

My Hustler September 1965

The Velvet Underground and *Nico: A Symphony of Sound*
January 1966

Chelsea Girls Summer 1966

The Andy Warhol Story Late 1966–67

**** (aka *Four Stars, The 25 Hour Movie,* and *The 24 Hour Movie*) 1966–67

The Loves of Ondine August 1967

Sunset Late 1967

Lonesome Cowboys Last week of January 1968

148   *Flesh* August–September 1968

Trash October 1969

Women in Revolt 1970–71

Heat June–July 1971

Andy Warhol's Frankenstein and *Andy Warhol's Dracula* March 1973

Warholstars Filmography by Gary Comenas, www.warholstars.org, 2002

books by andy warhol

A: A Novel. New York: Grove Press, 1968.

America. Photographs and text. New York: Harper & Row, 1985.

Andy Warhol's Exposures. Photographs with text by Andy Warhol and Bob Colacello. New York: Andy Warhol Books/Grosset and Dunlap, 1979.

Andy Warhol's Index Book. New York: Random House, 1967.

The Philosophy of Andy Warhol: From A to B and Back Again. New York: Harcourt Brace Jovanovich, 1975.

Andy Warhol's Party Book. With Pat Hackett. New York: Crown, 1988.

POPism: The Warhol Sixties. With Pat Hackett. New York: Harcourt Brace Jovanovich, 1980.

The Andy Warhol Diaries. Edited by Pat Hackett. New York: Warner Books, 1989.

glossary of artists and art terms

ABSTRACT: Used to describe paintings that present color, shape, line, or texture, rather than recognizable images.

ABSTRACT EXPRESSIONISM: A style of painting introduced by American artists (among them Jackson Pollock and Willem de Kooning) in the 1950s, with bold lines and splashes of color and usually no recognizable images. Also known as Action painters, these artists created the most important style of art in New York in the 1950s, when Andy Warhol moved there.

ACRYLIC: A type of fast-drying paint.

BASQUIAT, JEAN-MICHEL (1960–1988)**:** His graffiti-like images often refer to his Haitian and Puerto Rican heritage and demonstrate the artist's involvement with the urban environment. He and Andy collaborated on a series of paintings.

BLOTTED LINE: Using ink, Andy drew on glazed, nonabsorbent paper, then pressed the drawing onto an unglazed sheet. This transferred the ink outline, still wet, onto the softer paper and produced a scratchy, blotted effect.

BRUSHSTROKE: The mark made by a paintbrush.

CANVAS: The fabric on which an artist applies paint. Usually the canvas is stretched over a wooden frame and nailed into place.

COMMERCIAL ARTIST: A person who creates images to be used for advertising or for illustrating magazines or newspaper articles.

COMMON OBJECTS: Ordinary objects of daily life, such as soup cans or dollar bills, that became subjects of Andy's art.

COMPOSITION: The organization of the colors, lines, shapes, and textures in a painting. This general term refers to the relationship of the elements of art across the two-dimensional surface of a painting.

DINE, JIM (1935–)**:** Dine came into prominence in the 1960s in New York. In his paintings, drawings, collages, and sculpture, he combines different techniques with handwritten texts and single words and presents everyday objects, such as bathrobes and brooms, against undefined backgrounds. The objects are both commonplace and personal, reflecting his feelings about life.

151

DRAWING: A unique work of art made freehand in ink, chalk, pencil, or watercolor.

DUCHAMP, MARCEL (1887–1968)**:** The French painter, sculptor, and author was associated with such movements as Cubism, Surrealism, and Dadaism, although he avoided such labels. His work is characterized by humor, the use of a wide variety of materials, and a probing of the boundaries of art. His legacy includes the insight that art can be about anything, including ideas rather than objects—a notion that has influenced later generations of artists.

ELEMENTS OF ART: The basic parts of a painting—color, line, shape, and texture.

Color has three attributes: hue, intensity, and value. *Hue* refers to the six pure colors—red, orange, green, yellow, blue, and violet. *Intensity* refers to the brightness or dullness of a hue. *Value* refers to the lightness or darkness of a color.

Line refers to the mark the artist makes on a canvas. Lines outline a shape or connect one shape to another.

Shape and *form* refer to a particular area in a painting, such as a circle, a square, or a triangle.

Texture refers to the surface of a canvas, especially the way it stimulates our sense of touch.

EMPHASIS: One part of a painting dominating other parts to capture the viewer's attention, such as the large, bright heads in the centers of many of Andy's portraits.

FOUND IMAGE: An image or object that comes to the artist's attention by chance and is incorporated into an artwork, from an advertising image in a magazine to a stone or a man-made object. This comes from Surrealist theory, which holds that anything can be deemed a work of art by an artist.

GRAPHIC ARTIST: An artist who uses the silk-screen printing process, which allows him or her to repeat images.

GRID: A network of evenly spaced squares. In 1962, Andy

used rubber stamps to make gridded paintings, row upon row of repeated images, such as S&H Green Stamps.

HARING, KEITH (1958–1988)**:** He began drawing graffiti on subways in New York. His colorful sculpture, paintings, and drawings incorporate stick figures and animals. They have a playful, cartoonish quality.

INDIANA, ROBERT (1928–)**:** His early works were inspired by traffic signs, commercial stencils, and old trademarks. In the early sixties he created sculpture assemblages and developed his style of bold colored surfaces using words, letters, and numbers. He is associated with the Pop Art movement of the 1960s.

JOHNS, JASPER (1930–)**:** Johns, along with Rauschenberg, bridged the gap between Abstract Expressionism and Pop Art. He and Rauschenberg incorporated the free brushwork of the Abstract Expressionists into depictions of common objects. Johns used in his paintings such objects as a target, numbers, and the American flag.

LICHTENSTEIN, ROY (1923–1997)**:** Lichtenstein is famous for his brash paintings of comic strips, blown up and taken out of context, which explore the formal issues of painting and the ironies of contemporary life. Many of his paintings are adapted from those of other artists, reworked and simplified in bold two-dimensional forms.

MEDIUM: The material an artist works with—for example, photographs or pen and ink.

MODEL: A person who poses for an artist.

OLDENBURG, CLAES (1929–)**:** The Swedish artist came to prominence in New York in the 1960s both for his performance art, involving the creation of environments, and for his Pop Art sculpture of common objects in soft and hard materials. With his wife, Coosje van Bruggen, he later took up the fabrication of large-scale monuments, such as his *Lipstick* sculpture and *Clothespin,* as well as small-scale sculpture for parks and gardens.

PEARLSTEIN, PHILIP (1924–)**:** One of the leading realist painters of the second half of the twentieth century, Pearlstein painted both landscapes and figures at a time when abstract painting was fashionable. His dynamic studio paintings of nudes, against a background of strong patterns and textures, show scrupulous detail and are monumental in feeling. He and Andy both studied in Pittsburgh, and he was Andy's first roommate in New York.

PHOTOGRAPHIC SILK SCREEN: A photographic image is sent to a photo lab and transferred to a sheet of clear acetate. The craftsperson lays the sheet over a screen treated with light-sensitive material. The screen is developed by being exposed to a strong light, bringing out the photographic image. When the screen dries, it can be used in the same manner as a hand-cut stencil. Andy began using this method in 1962 for the Marilyn Series.

POLAROIDS: Instant photographs made with a Polaroid camera.

POLLOCK, JACKSON (1912–1956)**:** His large Abstract Expressionist paintings are considered the most influential of his generation. *Drip painting, action painting,* and *gestural painting* are some of the terms art critics and historians have applied to his canvases.

POP ART: The style of art made popular in the 1960s by such artists as Andy Warhol and Roy Lichtenstein, using images from such popular sources as advertising and comic books, and also using common objects such as soup cans and Coke bottles.

PORTRAIT: A painting of a person that is intended to give an impression of the person's appearance or personality.

PRIMARY COLORS: Red, yellow, or blue; in printing, magenta, yellow, and cyan.

RAUSCHENBERG, ROBERT (1925–)**:** This artist, whose interests extend beyond painting and sculpture to dance and stage design, explores the connections between art and life in his imaginative, experimental works.

REALISTIC ART: Art with a recognizable subject.

REPETITION: In Andy's paintings, repetition of his subjects, such as Elvis Presley or Marilyn Monroe, is employed to underline their use as consumer goods, their appeal to popular taste. Repetition is also used as a decorative device. Repeating patterns, colors, shapes, and lines is a way to create rhythm, unity, and balance in a composition.

REPRODUCTION: The production of multiple copies of an original work of art.

RHYTHM: Refers to the expression of movement in a painting by the repetition of colors, lines, shapes, or textures.

ROSENQUIST, JAMES (1933–)**:** Formerly a billboard painter, he creates bright, large-scale paintings, some incorporating magazine photographs, that explore commercialism and the industrialization of contemporary life.

SCALE: Size in an artwork, relative to the accepted, normal size of a person.

SCHARF, KENNY (1958–)**:** Along with Keith Haring and Jean-Michel Basquiat, Scharf placed his bright imagery, drawn from television and pop culture, on the streets and in the nightclubs of New York City. He calls his work Pop Surrealism because he believes his art comes from his unconscious, which is filled with pop imagery.

SCHNABEL, JULIAN (1951–)**:** He came into prominence in the 1980s in New York with his large-scale, bold paintings. In his best-known works, he incorporated broken plates and crockery, which were applied to vast wooden armatures. He is also a filmmaker and made a movie about the short, turbulent life of Jean-Michel Basquiat.

SELF-PORTRAIT: A portrait of the artist made by himself or herself.

SERIES: A group of artworks that are related by theme, subject matter, or medium.

SILK SCREEN: The process of printing by stretching a porous material, either silk or fine mesh screening, across a frame. The artist blocks out the areas he or she wishes to keep blank, lowers the screen over the paper or fabric to be imprinted, and with a squeegee (a rubber blade) forces ink through the uncovered portions of the screen. This is a negative-to-positive process, in that filled-in areas of the screen read as blank in the resulting image and the areas left open on the screen are covered with a layer of flat color.

STENCIL: When Andy selected an image (usually a preexisting photograph), he would send it to a commercial silk-screen shop to be transferred to a hand-cut stencil, a cutout replica of the image on strong, thick paper.

157

STILL LIFE: A painting of inanimate objects, such as flowers or soup cans.

SYMMETRY: Visual balance. A painting that is the same on both sides is called symmetrical.

VARIETY: Refers to the way artists use the elements of art, such as an array of shapes and colors, to provide contrast and visual interest. Andy, in his series work, gave each painting variety by using different color combinations and allowing for mistakes in the silk-screening process.

notes

Source abbreviations (complete citations appear in Sources)

Bok: Victor Bockris, *The Life and Death of Andy Warhol*.

Burns: Raw footage from The Andy Warhol Film Project. Producer Donald Rosenfeld. Director Ken Burns. Forthcoming.

Cola: Bob Colacello, *Holy Terror: Andy Warhol Close Up*.

Crone: Rainer Crone, *Andy Warhol,* translated by John William Gabriel.

David: David Bourdon, *Warhol*.

Edie: Jean Stein, *Edie: An American Biography,* edited with George Plimpton.

Essential: Ingrid Schaffner, *Andy Warhol,* The Essential Series.

EVO: *East Village Other.*

Factory: Steven Watson.

Factory Made: Factory Made: Warhol and the Sixties.

Mal: Gerard Malanga, *Archiving Warhol: An Illustrated History*.

Mirror: Kenneth Goldsmith, *I'll Be Your Mirror*.

Movie: Andy Warhol movie of the *Right Bank Show*.

Museum: *The Andy Warhol Museum*.

Notes: Jeanne Siegel, editor, *Art Talk: The Early 80s*.

NY: Paul Alexander, "What Happened to Andy's Treasures?" *New York Magazine*.

NYT: Ingrid Sischy, "Andy Land."

Own: *Andy Warhol in His Own Words*, edited by Mike Wrenn.

Pat: *Andy Warhol Diaries*, edited by Pat Hackett.

Philosophy: Andy Warhol, *The Philosophy of Andy Warhol: From A to B and Back Again*.

Pop: Andy Warhol and Pat Hackett, *POPism: The Warhol Sixties*.

PS: Patrick S. Smith, *Warhol: Conversations About the Artist*.

Tate: Bastian, Heiner, *Andy Warhol Retrospective*.

UV: Ultra Violet, *Famous for Fifteen Minutes: My Years with Andy Warhol*.

PITTSBURGH DAYS

Page 1.   *"I never wanted to be"*: Own, page 7.

Page 1.   *He loved her:* Bockris, who went to Pittsburgh in the 1980s and interviewed Andy's school friends and teachers, says that Warhol idolized Shirley Temple. His favorite movie was *Poor Little Rich Girl*. Bok, page 22.

Page 1.   *it would remain one of Andy's treasured possessions:* Shirley Temple's photograph was in Warhol's possession when he died. The photo is now part of the foundation's collection. Tate, page 288.

Page 2.   *"Being born," Andy later said, "is like . . .":* Philosophy, page 96.

Page 2.   *Andy came into the world:* Andy gave interviewers many different birthdates and places. He said, "I make it all up different every time I'm asked" (Own, page 6). He was able to do this since he was born at home and no actual birth certificate was issued until he went to college, at which time Julia Warhola had to swear an affidavit. The date she gave, August 6, 1928, is generally accepted.

Page 2.   *Andy shared a bed:* Description of family's living conditions from Burns, John Warhola interview.

Page 2.   *commercial television didn't exist:* The date accepted for the invention of television is 1927. Commercial television was launched at the 1939 World's Fair, though it didn't really get rolling until after the end of World War II.

Page 2.   *boys' games grew too rambunctious:* Burns, John Warhola interview.

Page 2.   *all three Warhola boys:* Paul was born in 1922; John was born in 1925.

Page 2.   *always won the giant Hershey bar:* Burns, John Warhola interview.

Page 3.   *"Someone hit a baseball . . . thought he was going to be a priest"; "Rain or shine there were no excuses":* Burns, John Warhola interview.

Page 3.   *three miles down a winding road:* Burns, John Warhola interview.

Page 3.   *"My mother . . . liked going to church":* Bok, page 13.

Page 3.   *Andy's family originated:* Warhol's ethnicity is not something that Andy has ever been quoted on directly. He occasionally said he was of Czechoslovakian ancestry—and indeed after World War I the Ruthenians voted to ally themselves with Czechoslovakia—but his family came from an area that has moved back and forth between several countries as borders changed but has its own ethnic identity. The subject is complicated, and there are divergent opinions. Paul Warhola, Andy's nephew, said that Carpatho-Rusyn or Ruthenian was preferred by his family. Among the Web sites dedicated to Carpatho-Rusyns and Ruthenians are www.halgal.com/ ruthenian.html and www.carpatho-rusynsociety.org/whoarerusyns.htm.

Page 4.   *three rivers meet:* The Allegheny River and the Monongahela River come together and form the Ohio River.

Page 4.   *the Great Depression:* The stock market crashed in October 1929. The depression that followed was the worst this country has ever seen. The unemployment rate sometimes reached 30 percent. The Great Depression didn't really end until the beginning of the Second World War.

Page 5. *various aunts, uncles, and cousins:* Julia had three brothers and two sisters living in or around Pittsburgh. Andrej also had a brother in the Pittsburgh area.

Page 5. *"She could really make you laugh":* Bok, page 15.

Page 5. *singing with the Gypsies:* Bok, page 7, and PS, page 127.

Page 6. *"Don't push him. He's too young yet":* Bok, page 15.

Page 6. *he spoke broken English:* Tate, page 287.

Page 6. *Margie Girman:* Bok, page 17.

Page 6. *"He was a good little artist":* Museum, page 148.

Pages 6–7. *"My dad couldn't afford to buy it":* Museum, page 148.

Page 7. *He caught rheumatic fever:* There are conflicting reports about what year or years Andy was sick, how sick he was, and how long he was ill. Some sources say he was eight years old, other sources say nine. Andy himself referred to "three nervous breakdowns," but he was not very reliable in the details of his recollections.

161

Page 7. *carry his kicking and shrieking brother:* Burns, John Warhola interview.

Page 8. *She put the family's only radio there:* Bockris says Julia moved the family's radio into his sickroom. Bourdon says the family didn't get one until Andy was eleven, after he was recovered.

Page 8. *house on Dawson Street:* Burns, John Warhola interview.

Page 9. *"From the class every week":* Museum, page 149.

Page 9. *"We used to show ourselves . . . warmed over":* Museum, pages 148–50.

Page 10. *"Art is not just a subject":* Museum, page 149.

Page 11.   *"I tried and tried"*: Philosophy, page 47.

Page 11.   *He preferred pretending:* Burns.

Page 12.   *Andy the red-nosed Warhola:* Philosophy, page 63.

Page 13.   *"I was captain of the . . . holding hands"*: Bok, page 55.

Page 13.   *"I wasn't amazingly popular"*: Philosophy, page 22.

Page 14.   *"It wasn't the sort of thing one thought about"*: Bok, page 65.

Page 14.   *"I didn't want them to have the same problems I did"*:
Philosophy, page 46.

Page 14.   *her only chance was a risky new operation:* Julia had an
operation in which a section of the bowels is removed and a bag to
collect their waste material is attached to the patient's abdomen. Andy
later wanted Julia to have this corrected, but she refused to go back
into the hospital.

162

Page 15.   *whose seventeenth birthday occurred only a few weeks:*
Bockris says Andy skipped fourth grade; other sources say fifth. He
also finished high school in three years because schools were acceler-
ating their programs so that eighteen-year-olds, who were eligible for
the draft, could graduate before they went into the armed services.
Museum, pages 50–51.

Page 15.   *Instead he chose the smaller Carnegie Tech:* The full
name at that time was the Carnegie Institute of Technology.
Originally founded in 1900 by Andrew Carnegie, a Pittsburgh indus-
trialist, Carnegie Tech merged with the Mellon Institute of Science
in 1967 to become Carnegie Mellon University. Museum, page 151.

WHY PICK ON ME?

Page 16.   *"artists are never"*: Own, page 8.

Page 16.   *for some . . . it was Judgment Day:* Museum, page 153.

Page 16.   *"I created a big scene and cried"*: David, page 20.

Page 17.   *Philip Pearlstein:* Pearlstein is a realistic painter (mostly of nudes) who has had his own distinguished art career.

Page 17.   *"It was very apparent":* Bok, page 39.

Page 17.   *"If anyone would have asked me":* Quote from Robert Lepper, who taught a course in pictorial design at Carnegie Tech. David, page 21.

Page 17.   *"I want you to give this kid another chance":* Museum, page 153.

Page 17.   *"Damn it, you just must stop drawing":* PS, pages 13–14.

Page 18.   *"He used to sell the drawings"* . . . *The suprised reaction was "Andy Warhola did these?":* PS, page 14.

Page 18.   *"Andy was a very young person":* Bok, page 39.

Page 19.   *Andy turned in a splat* . . . *"It's supposed to be blood":* Museum, page 157.

Page 20.   *Joseph Horne:* This was the premier department store in downtown Pittsburgh in the days when shopping was an event and women dressed up to go shopping downtown.

163

Page 20.   *"homosexuality was pretty well accepted in art school":* Bok, page 41.

Pages 20–21.   *The Broad Gave Me My Face:* This story is told in several places, including Museum, page 164, and PS, page 16.

Page 21.   *"He was never argumentative":* Leonard Kessler, a well-known and successful children's book writer and illustrator, went to Carnegie Tech with Andy, and he and his wife were Andy's friends both there and later in the early days in New York. He is the source of this comment. Bok, page 39.

Page 21.   *"Andy, just believe in destiny":* David, page 22.

Page 22   *"I loved working":* Philosophy, page 96.

Page 22.   *To his dismay, a cockroach crept from between the pages:* Andy told this story several times as having happened to him, e.g., Philosophy, page 23. Philip Pearlstein claims that he, not Andy, was the unlucky bearer of a roach, and that the editor gave him the boot, not the job. Cola, page 21.

Page 23.   *Philip told him, "Brush your hair! Put on a suit":* Bok, page 52.

Page 23.   *Raggedy Andy:* Bok, page 52.

Page 23.   *"I greeted a pale, blotchy boy":* Essential, page 29.

Page 24.   *he had planted some birdseed:* This story was told by several people, including two of his assistants, Joseph Groell (PS, page 30) and Nathan Gluck (PS, page 68).

Page 25.   *"I kept living with roommates thinking we could become good friends":* Philosophy, page 22.

Page 25.   *"a workaholic who sat at a table":* Bok, page 53.

Page 26.   *McCarthy hearings:* From 1950 to 1954, building on the investigations started by the House Un-American Activities Committee, Senator Joseph McCarthy actively pursued Communists, homosexuals, and other "deviants," whom he represented as a threat to United States security. In 1953 and 1954 he held hearings in the Senate. People appearing before the committee were asked, "Are you now, or have you ever been, a member of the Communist Party?" At the slightest hint of suspicion, your name could be placed on a blacklist, which would effectively prevent anyone from hiring you. More than 320 people in the entertainment industry were placed on such lists (without a trial). Many others, including teachers, military personnel, and government employees, also were blacklisted. *McCarthyism* is now used as a synonym for a witch hunt, but at the time Andy moved to New York it was a genuine threat.

Page 26.   *"One day my mother . . . Just a hopeless, born loser":*

Truman Capote (1924–1984) was an author who became famous at age twenty-four for his book *Other Voices, Other Rooms,* with its daring (for the time) depiction of homosexuality. Other books include *Breakfast at Tiffany's* (1958) and *In Cold Blood* (1966). Edie, page 196.

MAKING IT

Page 28. *"My mother was a wonderful woman":* Own, page 6.

Page 28. *ice cream truck:* Told in Bok, page 66.

Page 29. *Hugo Gallery:* David, page 32.

Pages 29–30. *handmade, limited-edition books: A Is an Alphabet,* with Ralph (Corkie) Ward providing the minimal text to go with Andy's illustrations, was the first of the books. PS, page 125.

Page 30. *I. Miller:* Geraldine Stutz, then the head of I. Miller's retail division, quoted in PS, pages 101–3.

Page 31. *Carl Willers:* The relationship is discussed by Carl Willers (called Walters) in PS, pages 143–48, and Bok, pages 73–74. According to Bockris, Andy and Carl were friends for about ten years but lovers for only a brief time.

Page 31. *"Andy, this is insane":* David, page 30.

Page 32. *"I am Andy Warhol":* PS, page 127.

Page 32. *Serendipity 3:* PS, page 148.

Page 33. *"He used to be the strangest little guy":* PS, page 133.

Page 33. *Charles took home movies of Andy:* PS, page 134.

Page 33. *"Up to that point, Andy was . . . sweet, gentle and shy":* PS, page 123.

Page 34. *"You would make a good wife for my Andy":* David, page 68. Andy's nephew James Warhola says that not only Julia but the whole Warhola family were unaware that Andy was gay. It didn't occur to them, partly because there were so many women art directors around, and later because he always was having his photograph taken with glamorous women. Author interview.

Pages 34–35. *"He submitted a group of boys kissing boys . . . probably the last time we were in touch":* Edie, page 188. Even though Pearlstein says that was the last time they were in touch, they remained friendly enough that James Warhola, Andy's nephew, remembers running into Pearlstein while at the Museum of the City of New York with his uncle, and recalls that the two men chatted for about a half hour. Author interview.

Page 35. *"Okay, Andy, if you really want to hear it straight . . . You're famous for it":* Pop, pages 11–12.

Page 35. *Jackson Pollock:* Andy arrived in New York when Jackson Pollock (1912–1956) was at the height of his powers and had been dubbed the greatest painter in America. Jackson died in an automobile accident in 1956, but his influence was still widely felt.

Page 35. *Andy couldn't imagine himself in this tough, two-fisted, mostly male world:* Pop, page 15.

POP!

Page 37. *"The Pop artists did images":* Pop, page 39.

Page 37. *A small drawing of a lightbulb!:* Pop, page 6.

Page 37. *Leo Castelli Gallery:* Leo Castelli (1907–1999) was a dealer whose keen eye and impeccable taste made him one of the most influential figures in contemporary art. His galleries, first uptown and later in Soho, were vital in introducing this art to the public.

Page 38. *"Oh, I'm doing work just like that":* David, page 80.

Page 39. *"I was getting paid for it":* G. R. Swenson, "What Is Pop Art?" *Artnews*, November 1963, page 26.

Page 39. *When Karp arrived at Andy's studio:* PS, page 38.

Page 39. *"You should do more paintings like this":* Movie.

Page 40.   *Karp convinced his boss to take a look at Andy's work:* Ivan Karp was respected in art circles for his good eye. Part of his job at Castelli was to look at the slides of the work of new artists who wanted to join the gallery. If he liked what he saw, he might make a studio visit to look at the paintings. Critics, collectors, and other people interested in contemporary art sometimes asked Karp for recommendations so they could visit artists and see the work even before the artist had an official gallery.

Page 40.   *There was no room in the gallery, Castelli said:* Nearly fifty years later, when viewers are used to Pop Art, we can see that the work of Warhol and Lichtenstein doesn't look alike, but in the beginning of the movement, because both artists were inspired by subjects taken from popular culture, the dealer feared that their work looked too similar and that Warhol's work would compete with Lichtenstein, whom he already represented.

Page 41.   *"It was like a science fiction movie":* Pop, page 3.

Page 41.   *"What should I paint?":* David, page 87.

Page 42.   *"I can give you an idea . . .":* Story told by Andy's friend Ted Carey. PS, pages 90–91.

167

SOUP CANS AND CELEBRITIES

Page 43.   *"Pop art is for everyone".* EVO.

Page 43.   *Irving Blum:* The word was out that Andy was talented, and Blum had been to visit him once before, sent by Ivan Karp. David, page 86.

Page 44.   *"The paintings were vividly assaulted":* Movie.

Page 44.   *Get the real thing for 29 cents:* PS, page 195.

Page 44.   *"I just paint things I always thought were beautiful":* Time, May 11, 1962.

Page 46.   *"Warhol's paintings are potentially reproducible":* Crone, page 10.

Page 46.   *"I think somebody should be able to do all my paintings for me":* Crone, page 10.

Page 47.   *"Pop art was really an obsession . . .":* Edie, page 199.

Page 47.   *he gave his mother, Julia, her own apartment:* Several of Andy's friends said Julia drank, but it seems to have been on account of Andy's remark that she drank a case of Cutty Sark a week, since after a while only a few of them saw much of her and no one reports having seen her drunk. Julia's grandson James Warhola says his grandmother did not drink, and her garden apartment was the coziest and most comfortable room in the house. Author interview with James Warhola.

Page 49.   *"five-hours-a-day-on-the-phone":* Pop, page 16.

Page 49.   *"129 Die in Jet Crash":* David, page 118.

Pages 49–50.   *"No matter how good you are":* Pop, page 21.

Page 50.   *"I was lying there on my back":* PS, page 200.

Page 50.   *"Well, I'll give you a show":* De told this story (PS, page 189) and Andy told it (Pop, page 24).

Page 51.   *"Have you seen the Andy Warhol show?":* Eleanor Ward is the source of this story about Bill Seitz and Peter Selz, two directors of the Museum of Modern Art, known around town at that time as the Bobbsey Twins. PS, page 202.

FAME!

Page 52.   *"In the future":* Andy Warhol, Stockholm: Moderna Musee, 1968, MOMA.

Page 52.   *"I really don't know what to say . . . being in a Western movie":* Movie.

Page 53.   *Andy was not the only artist who avoided discussing his intentions:* For example, Georgia O'Keeffe said she could say things with color and shapes that she had no words for. And Edward Hopper famously told people who asked about the meaning that the answer was in the paintings.

Page 53.   *Whether the public loved it or hated it:* Own, page 22.

Page 53.   *"The things I want to show are mechanical":* Time, May 20, 1963.

Page 54.   *"he's [Robert Scull] the oddest figure":* Pop, page 67.

Page 54.   *Ethel, fresh from the hairdresser:* The description of taking Ethel Scull's portrait is from David, pages 158–60.

Page 55.   *"The image . . . a . . . face, . . . lips":* Mal, page 104.

Page 56.   *Finally he realized who his employer was:* Discussion of this first meeting is in a memoir Gerard wrote of his time with Andy. Mal, pages 19, 32, 105.

Page 56.   *"If you were to meet him for the first time":* Mal, page 47.

Pages 56–57.   *"Each painting . . . 'It's just part of the art.' ":* Bok, page 170.

Page 57.   *"I realized everything I was doing must be death":* Bok, page 169.

169

Page 57.   *"He would never never never never say that it has a meaning":* Crone, page 10.

Page 57.   *"Andy pretends he has no politics.":* Crone, page 11.

Page 58.   *"The more you look at the exact same thing":* Pop, page 50.

Page 58.   *"The [Disaster] pictures become holy scenes":* Bok, page 129.

Page 58.   *"Especially if the background matches the drapes":* Philosophy, page 18.

Page 59.   *"What held his work together":* Bok, page 171.

Page 59.   *"I'm not a social critic":* Bok, page 170.

Page 59.   *"I don't believe in love"* and *"I want to be a machine"*: David, page 140.

MADE IN AMERICA

Page 60.   *"I like boring things"*: MOMA, page 457.

Page 60.   *"How terrible"*: Bok, page 176.

Pages 60–61.   *"What are you doing?"* . . . *"I want to make a movie of you sleeping"*: Bok, page 177.

Page 62.   *"Many a big shot guy in the sky might die"*: PS, page 183.

Page 62.   *"The farther west we drove"*: Pop, page 39.

Page 62.   *Hollywood*: Pop, pages 40–45.

Page 63.   *"If you take a Campbell's Soup can"*: Bok, page 159.

Page 63.   *"Even when the Pop Art explosion happened"*: NYT.

170   Page 64.   *"So what"*: Philosophy, page 112.

THE SWINGING SILVER FACTORY

Page 66.   *"A lot of people thought"*: Pop, page 100.

Page 66.   *"Silver was the future"*: Pop, page 64.

Page 67.   *"It became a sort of glamorous clubhouse"*: Edie, page 201.

Page 69.   *"The work was to us very impressive"*: PS, page 321.

Page 69.   *"Apparently,"* Andy said, *"most people like watching the same basic thing"*: Pop, page 50.

Page 69.   *"If you want to know all about Andy Warhol"*: Bok, page 196.

Page 70.   *"Well,"* said Andy, *"let's replace it with pictures of the head of the fair"*: Bok, page 150.

Page 70. *"I want it to look like a warehouse":* Bok, page 198; David, pages 182–83.

Page 71. *brought the history of Western art to a close:* Arthur Danto, quoted in the *New York Observer,* September 15, 2003, page 20.

THE PRINCE OF POP

Page 72. *"Don't think about making art":* Own, page 22.

Page 72. *"a muscle man's S&M black leather jacket":* Bok, page 195.

Page 73. *"The Factory," Andy said, "was a place where":* Wrenn, page 36.

Page 74. *"It will be an ear-catcher":* UV, page 81.

Page 74. *"That's the torn look":* UV, page 83.

Page 74. *Superstars:* In Philosophy, page 26, Andy gives credit to the Jersey girl who renamed herself Ingrid Superstar (real name Ingrid von Scheven) for inventing the Superstar designation. In an interview in *High Times,* Andy credits Jack Smith (Flaming Creatures).

Page 75. *she also was designated the first Girl of the Year:* Baby Jane Holzer was the subject of Tom Wolfe's essay "The Girl of the Year" in his best-selling book *The Kandy-Kolored Tangerine-Flake Streamline Baby* (New York: Farrar, Straus, and Giroux, 1965).

Page 75. *Screen Tests:* These are now being curated, restored, and shown in a joint project of the Warhol Museum and the Whitney Museum.

Page 76. *"creating cliques and setting up rivalries":* Pat, page xix.

Page 76. *"I feel wonderfully liberated":* UV, pages 109–10.

Page 77. *"It was a rough democracy":* Burns, interview with Dave Hickey.

Page 77. *"Enough death and disaster":* Bok, page 209.

Page 77. *He found a photograph of seven hibiscus blossoms:* Andy used a photograph for the flower paintings without bothering to clear permissions. The photographer sued him, and eventually he settled with her by giving her several of the paintings. PS, page 217. After that experience Andy tended to take his own photographs instead of using other people's pictures.

Page 78. *"Andy is in a sense a victim of common things":* Bok, page 210.

Page 78. *"She shot my paintings!":* Bok, page 149. Ondine tells the story in Edie on page 208, but he says it was Harriet Teacher instead of Dorothy Podber.

POOR LITTLE RICH GIRL

Page 80. *"The two girls I used most in my films":* EVO/Mirror, page 82.

Page 80. *"the best legs in New York":* Pop, page 109.

Page 81. *"Edie would be innovating her own look":* Pop, page 109.

Page 81. *"Edie was incredible on camera":* Pop, page 109.

Page 81. *"Glamour she inhales":* UV, page 205.

Page 82. *"You just fell in love with her":* Danny Fields in PS, page 286.

Page 82. *"Art,"* he wrote later, *"just wasn't fun":* Pop, page 112.

Page 82. *All the publicity made her famous, but she wasn't earning any money:* Bok, page 173.

Page 83. *"My Hustler was the first full-length film":* David, page 261.

Page 83. *"We want Andy and Edie!":* Edie, page 254.

Page 83. *"We weren't just at the art exhibit":* Edie, page 255.

Pages 83–84. *The rest of his friends . . . feared for their safety:* The story of the events in Philadelphia are from David, page 214, and Edie, pages 253–55.

Page 84. *"Now and then people would accuse me of being evil"*: Pop, page 108.

Page 84. *"You can't make them change if they don't want to"*: Pop, page 108.

Page 85. *"an extreme prude making x-rated movies"*: Cola, page 35.

THE VELVET UNDERGROUND

Page 86. *"Publicity is like eating peanuts"*: Own, page 54.

Page 86. *a band called the Velvet Underground:* Members of the Velvet Underground were Maureen (Mo) Tucker, percussion; John Cale, bass; Sterling Morrison, lead guitar; and Lou Reed, songwriter and lead singer.

Page 87. *"wind in a drainpipe"*: Pop, page 145.

Page 87. *"a real moon goddess type"*: Bok, page 241.

Page 87. *New York Society of Clinical Psychologists:* David, page 221.

173

Page 88. *Radical chic, . . . Tom Wolfe called it.:* Tom Wolfe wrote two articles, "Those Radical Chic Evenings" and "Mau-Mauing the Flak Catchers," that eventually were published in a book called, not too surprisingly, *Radical Chic and Mau-Mauing the Flak Catchers* (New York: Farrar, Straus, and Giroux, 1970). In them he skewered the Park Avenue socialites earnestly hobnobbing with Black Panthers, and the confrontation tactics of the newly politicized black community dealing with the middle class bureaucracy. The articles are satiric, but they also are profoundly insightful about aspects of American life in the late sixties.

Page 88. *The Exploding Plastic Inevitable:* This was Andy's new name for the Velvets and the light show. David, page 225.

Page 89. *Drella:* Andy's nickname may have been given to him by Ondine.

Page 89. *Andy's venture into rock and roll fizzled out:* Lou Reed said even though they had a contract Andy didn't try to hold him to it. He just called him a rat and let him go. PS, page 86.

Page 89.   *"There was an aching poverty"*: PS, page 185.

Page 89.   *"bring home the bacon"*: This was one of Andy's pet phrases. "Someone has to bring home the bacon," he'd say. Brigid Berlin quotes him in Burns.

Page 90.   *Venice Biennale*: David, page 226.

CHELSEA GIRLS

Page 91.   *"Scripts bore me"*: Own, page 33.

Page 91.   *"I love hotels to which at four a.m."*: See Christof Graf, "Leonard Cohen's Chelsea Hotel at Midnight," www.leonardcohenfiles.com/chelsea.html.

Page 92.   "You fool": This exists in many clips. Ondine discussed the making of the scene in Movie.

Page 93.   *Brigid Berlin reported that after her very proper mother:* Burns.

Page 93.   *"Those movies showed you how some people act and react"*: Own, page 30.

Pages 93–94.   *Max's Kansas City:* General description from www.maxskansascity.com.

Page 94.   *"If I liked somebody"*: www.maxskansascity.com.

Page 94.   *Jimi Hendrix said:* www.maxskansascity.com.

ENTER FRED HUGHES

Page 95.   *"You get to a point in life"*: Factory Made, page 305.

Page 95.   *Viva:* Viva, real name Susan Hoffman, was a nice girl from a good family in upstate New York. She became one of Andy's most popular and outrageous Superstars.

Page 96.   *"Uh, well, we just did it"*: David, page 289.

Page 97.   *"I'm deeply superficial"*: Cola, page 94.

Page 97.   *"Fred," Andy said, "is really up there"*: Cola, page 52.

Page 98.   *"Maybe I should just shoot a cactus for thirty-five minutes"*: David, page 275.

Page 98.   *"Your line was no good anyway"*: David, page 276.

Page 99.   *"Now that Boris Karloff and Bela Lugosi have passed on"*: David, page 301.

SHOT!

Page 100.   *"I was in the wrong place"*: Movie.

Page 100.   *She looked harmless:* Almost everyone who was at the Factory at the time of the shooting talked and/or wrote about it afterward. Eyewitness accounts usually vary, and while the outline is the same, the details differ.

Page 100.   *"It was so dirty"*: Pop, page 271.

Page 100.   *he offered her twenty-five dollars for a day's work:* Valerie was good in the film, funny and feisty.

Page 101.   *When Andy and Jed Johnson encountered Valerie that summer day:* Valerie had gone up to the Factory looking for Andy, and Paul Morrissey told her she couldn't hang around, so she waited on the street. Jed had been doing errands and just happened to be arriving at the same time as Andy.

Page 101.   *Midnight Cowboy:* Andy and Paul Morrissey thought Hollywood had ripped off *My Hustler*.

Page 101.   *"No! No! Valerie!"*: Pop, page 273.

Page 101.   *He thought a sniper was shooting at them:* Edie, page 289.

Page 101.   *"Valerie shot Andy"*: Bok, page 299.

Page 101.   *"Please don't shoot me, Valerie":* Bok, page 228. Initially Fred thought the shooting had something to do with the Communist Party, which had offices on another floor of the building (Bok, page 227). Did Valerie hold a gun to Fred's head? Some accounts say yes, some no.

Page 102.   *"Oh, please don't make me laugh, Billy":* Pop, page 273; Bok, page 300.

Page 102.   *"For an extra fifteen dollars":* Edie, page 290.

Page 102.   *"Forget it":* Pop, page 274.

Page 102.   *"It's Andy Warhol":* Bok, page 231.

Page 102.   *The bullets had nicked:* The bullets passed through his lung, esophagus, gallbladder, liver, spleen, and intestines, and he lost most of his blood. For the rest of his life Andy had to wear a corset to keep his insides from pooching out when he ate. He probably never felt completely well again, though he was stoic about his pain.

176   Page 103.   *"Why did they shoot my Andy?":* Bok, page 233.

Page 103.   *Ultra later confessed to feeling a little self-conscious:* UV, page 177.

Page 103.   *"He had too much control over my life":* Bok, page 232.

Pages 103–104.   *"The Pop art king was the blond guru of a nightmare world":* Andy, who courted the press and never corrected their stories even when they were inaccurate, later said that this story in *Time* was "the worst, most cruel review of me" that he ever read. Philosophy, page 78.

Page 104.   *a Daily News columnist moralized:* UV, page 178.

Page 104.   *Robert Kennedy's assassination:* Pop, page 274.

Page 104.   *"The fear of getting shot again":* Pop, page 279.

Page 105.   *Andy continued to feel afraid to be alone:* Pop, page 284.

Page 105.   *"Andy expected everyone who worked for him to do their job":* Pat, xii.

Page 106.   *"Andy, I am not here":* Pop, page 300.

INTERVIEW

Page 107.   *"I hate subscriptions":* David, page 303.

Page 107.   *Interview:* The title of *Interview* changed through the years. It began as *Inter/VIEW,* changed to *Andy Warhol's Interview*, and finally became *Interview*. We've used the present spelling throughout.

Page 107.   *Bob Colacello:* Colacello wrote *Holy Terror: Andy Warhol Close Up* (New York: HarperCollins, 1990), an amusing account of his days at the Factory, now renamed the Office, working for Andy in various capacities.

Pages 107–108.   *"Putting together a magazine":* Cola, page 37.

Page 108.   *"Andy wanted to be like Walt Disney":* PS, page 171.

Page 108.   *"Let's combine the two ideas":* Cola, page 5.

Pages 108–109.   *drag queen:* Pat, xiv.

Page 109.   *Poetry, he said, was not "modern":* Cola, page 44.

Page 109.   *Andy brought his "wife, Sony":* Andy said, "I didn't get married until 1964 when I got my first tape recorder. My wife. My tape recorder and I have been married for ten years now." Philosophy, page 26.

Page 109.   *"Talking to Andy":* Cola, page 109.

Page 109.   *"The interviews can be funny":* Cola, page 255.

Page 110.   *"we retouch anyone over the age of twenty":* Pat, page xvi.

Page 111.   *"whereas the people we use, think they really are women":* Movie.

Page 111. *"Candy was the most striking drag queen":* Pop, page 226.

Page 112. *since* Interview *wasn't actually making money:* Cola, page 59.

Page 113. *"Have you popped the question yet?":* "Fred was always popping the question then, and more often than not getting yes for an answer. That was the basis of his power at the Factory: He brought home the most bacon by far." Cola, page 168.

Page 113. *"Warhol portraits were like Warhol interviews":* Burns.

PUTTING MY ANDY ON

Page 114. *"I don't get too close":* EVO/Mirror, page 88.

Page 114. *"All those beautiful people coming in the house":* David, page 308.

Page 115. *Mrs. Warhola had lost touch with reality:* Bok, pages 350–52; David, page 308.

Page 115. *"glue":* Pat, page xviii.

Page 115. *retrospective at the Whitney Museum:* Cola, pages 62–65.

Page 116. *"The plain inescapable fact":* Bok, page 259.

Page 116. *"fresh and brilliant . . . cruel clarity":* Cola, pages 64–65.

Page 116. *"the man on the* Sticky Fingers *album cover":* Bok, page 346.

Page 117. *"I've been reading so much about China":* David, page 317.

Page 118. *"Don't tell anyone," he warned them:* The Tate Museum Warhol catalog contains a transcription of one of Andy's taped phone calls with his brother at the time of his mother's death in which he warns them to keep it a secret. Tate, pages 32–33.

Page 118. *"Fine. She doesn't get out much":* David, page 322.

ANDY WARHOL ENTERPRISES

Page 121.   *"Buying is much more American":* Philosophy, page 229.

Page 121.   *"People should fall in love with their eyes closed":* Philosophy, page 50.

Page 121.   *"Money is the moment":* Philosophy, page 136.

Page 122.   *Time Capsules:* The Web site of the Warhol Museum is www.warhol.org. They have a long piece on the Time Capsules, including lists of things taken from the capsules that have been opened.

Page 123.   *Shadow paintings:* PS, page 354; Pat, page 199.

Page 123.   *"Oh, that looks so pretty!":* PS, page 349.

Page 124.   *"I don't want to live forever":* David, page 360.

THE LAST YEARS

Page 125.   *"I go to a small Roman Catholic":* Movie.

Page 125.   *Jean-Michel Basquiat:* The diaries that cover the last years of Andy's life detail his artistic involvement with and personal concern for Basquiat.

Page 127.   *"Business art is the step that comes after Art":* Philosophy, page 92; Pop, page 190.

Page 127.   *"making money is art":* Philosophy, page 92.

Page 128.   *"What could be more wicked":* NYT.

Page 128.   *"He lost steam in the last few years":* Burns.

Page 129.   *"Do you have any masterpieces?":* NY, page 28.

Page 129.   *Andy didn't show his treasure trove to anyone:* Cola, page 241.

Page 130. *"I paint pictures of myself":* Bok, page 480.

Pages 131–132. *"If visitors can't get in":* Museum, page 191.

Page 133. *"Posterity may well decide":* NYT.

POSTSCRIPT

Page 134. *"When I die":* Own, page 93.

sources

BOOKS

The Andy Warhol Museum. Angel, Callie, Avis Berman, et al., New York: Art Publishers, Inc. 1994.

Bockris, Victor. *Warhol*. London: Da Capo Press, 1997.

Bourdan, David. *Warhol.* New York: Harry N. Abrams, 1989.

Colacello, Bob. *Holy Terror: Andy Warhol Close Up.* New York: Cooper Square Press, 1990.

Crone, Rainer. *Andy Warhol: The Early Works 1942–1962.* New York: Praeger, 1970.

Goldsmith, Kenneth. *I'll Be Your Mirror: The Selected Andy Warhol Interviews, 1962–1987.* New York: Carroll & Graf, 2004.

Heiner, Bastian. *Andy Warhol Retrospective.* London: Tate Publishing and Museum of Contemporary Art, Los Angeles, 2001.

Honnef, Klaus. *Warhol (1928–1987): Commerce Into Art.* Cologne: Taschen, 2000.

McShine, Kynaston, ed. *Andy Warhol: A Retrospective*. New York: Museum of Modern Art, 1989.

Malanga, Gerard. *Archiving Warhol: An Illustrated History*. New York: Creation Books, 2002.

Ratcliff, Carter. *Warhol*. Modern Masters Series. New York: Abbeville Press, 1983.

Schaffner, Ingrid. *The Essential Andy Warhol*. New York: Wonderland Press, 1999.

Siegel, Jeanne, ed. *Art Talk: The Early '80's*. New York: Da Capo, 1990.

Smith, John W., ed. *Possession Obsession*: *Andy Warhol and Collecting*. Pittsburgh: Andy Warhol Museum, 2002.

Smith, Patrick S. *Warhol: Conversations About the Artist*. Ann Arbor: UMI Research Press, 1988.

Stein, Jean, ed., with George Plimpton. *Edie: An American Biography*. New York: Knopf, 1982.

Violet, Ultra, aka Isabel Dufresne. *Famous for Fifteen Minutes: My Years with Andy Warhol*. New York: Harcourt, Brace, Jovanovich, 1988.

Watson, Steven. *Factory Made: Warhol and the Sixties*. New York: Pantheon, 2003.

Woronov, Mary. *Swimming Underground: My Years in the Warhol Factory*. London: Serpent's Tail, 2002.

Wrenn, Mike, ed. *Andy Warhol in His Own Words*. London: Omnibus Press, 1991.

ARTICLES

Alexander, Paul. "What Happened to Andy's Treasures?" *New York* magazine, January 27, 1992.

La Furla, Ruth. "Together Again, That Colorful Couple, Art and Fashion." *The New York Times,* Arts, September 30, 2003.

Sischy, Ingrid. "Andy Land," *Fashions of the Times, The New York Times*, August 17, 2003.

FILMS

Andy Warhol, London Weekend Television (South Bank Show), 1987.

Ric Burns, Raw Footage for *The Andy Warhol Project,* produced by Donald Rosenfeld.

photography credits

Reproductions are by permission of the owners of the original works, who supplied color transparencies and black-and-white photographs, except in the following cases:

Untitled (cat from *25 Cats Name Sam and One Blue Pussy*)
Anyone for Shoes?
Large Coca-Cola
129 Die in Jet (Plane Crash)
Double Mona Lisa
Liz
Electric Chair
Elvis I & II
16 Jackies
Muhammad Ali
Vote McGovern
Hammer & Sickle
Skull
Exhibition poster for the Andy Warhol/Jean-Michel Basquiat show at the Tony Shafrazi Gallery, New York
$9

All of the above photographs are from The Andy Warhol Foundation, Inc./Art Resource, NY.

Ethel Scull 36 Times/Photograph by Geoffrey Clements/Whitney Museum of American Art, NY.

Shadows/Photograph by Bill Jacobson/Collection Dia Art Foundation.

acknowledgments

We would like to thank John Smith and Matt Wrbican at the Andy Warhol Museum for reading and advising; Donald Rosenfeld, the producer of the Andy Warhol Film Project, for his openhanded sharing of the footage for the forthcoming film; James Warhola, who spoke to us about his visits to his uncle; and Wendy Worth for personal memories of Andy. Thank you to Amy Kellman from the Carnegie Library, who paused in her busy day to research and clarify some important questions about the Carnegie Institute in Pittsburgh. Gael Neeson and Stefan Edlis, and the Greenberg Van Doren Gallery, generously loaned transparencies of Andy's artworks. Jane and Marc Nathanson and Lynda and Stewart Resnick were our hosts for the opening of the Warhol retrospective at MOCA, the Museum of Contemporary Art in Los Angeles, and Linda and Chris Davis hosted our visit to the Warhol retrospective at the Tate Modern in London. Thank you also to Jackie Greenberg; Jeanne Greenberg Rohatyn; Matthew Lore; Ralph Elia; our agent, George Nicholson; and his assistant, Paul Rodeen, all of whom contributed wit, time, space, and encouragement to our undertaking. And we are, as always, grateful to the talented people who take our manuscript and turn it into a book: our serene editor, Françoise Bui; vigilant copy editor Barbara Perris; agreeable designer Kenny Holcomb; Joe Cooper for the jacket concept and expert handling of complicated permissions; astute indexer Alison Kolani; admirable production person Melissa Fariello; and last but never least, Tamar Schwartz, who mysteriously keeps things flowing in a timely fashion.

index

A Is an Alphabet, 30

A la Recherche du Shoe Perdu, 30

Abstract Expressionism, 35–36, 38, 39, 41, 45, 53

Amaya, Mario, 101, 102, 103

America, Paul, 83

Andy Warhol Enterprises, 101, 108, 112

Andy Warhol Foundation, 136–137

Andy Warhol Museum, 122, 136–137

Animals: Species at Risk, 130

Antonio, Emile de. *see* De

Avedon, Richard, 104

Bad, 119

Bailey, David, 111, 114

Bardot, Brigitte, 94

Basquiat, Jean-Michel, 125–126, 127–128, 135

Beatty, Warren, 46

Beauty #2, 81

Berlin, Brigid (aka Brigid Polk), 74, 85, 92, 93, 115, 119, 120, 131, 135

Bischofberger, Bruno, 116–117, 125

Blum, Irving, 43–44, 61

Brillo Boxes, 70–71, 78, 137

Broad Gave Me My Face but I Can Pick My Own Nose, The, 20–21

Campbell's soup can paintings, 43–44, 45, 49, 50, 51, 56, 63, 116, 127, 130, 137

Canaday, John, 116

Canby, Vincent, 118

Cannes Film Festival, 94

Capote, Truman, 26–27, 29, 34, 113, 125

Carnegie Institute of Technology, 8–9, 14–21, 25

Carpatho-Ruthenia, 3–4, 5–6

Carter, Jimmy, 113

Castelli, Leo, 40, 41, 71, 83, 102, 103, 134. *see also* Leo Castelli Gallery

Catholicism, 3, 85, 104,
110, 132, 135
Chamberlain, John, 93
Chamberlain, Win, 61
Chelsea Girls, 91–93, 94,
96, 97
Close, Chuck, 93–94
Cohen, Leonard, 91
Coke bottle paintings, 39,
45, 49, 53
Colacello, Bob, 107–110,
113, 119, 131
comic books, 7, 38, 52
Communism, 26, 117,
122–123
Couch, 67
Cow Wallpaper, 115–116
Cowboys and Indians,
130
Crone, Rainer, 46
Cunningham, Merce, 90
Curtis, Jackie, 110, 111,
118
Cutrone, Ronnie, 122, 123

Dallesandro, Joe, 110, 111,
118
Danto, Arthur, 71
Darling, Candy, 111, 115,
118
da Vinci, Leonardo, 55, 131
De, 35, 36, 50, 54, 57–58

de Menil, John and
Dominique, 96, 97
Disaster Series, 56–59, 64,
116, 137
Dom, the, 88–89
Donahue, Troy, 46, 62
Dracula, 119
drugs, 59, 66, 73, 74, 77,
82, 84, 85, 92, 96, 127,
128
Duchamp, Marcel, 62–63
Dylan, Bob, 84, 89, 91, 94

Easy Rider, 62
Eat, 68
Electric Chair, 58

Factory, the, 65, 72, 75, 80,
83, 84, 93, 96, 97, 101,
102, 103, 104, 105,
108, 110, 113, 115,
119, 120, 125, 126,
128, 129, 134, 135, 136
as art, film, and music
studio, 70, 77, 85,
86–87, 92
design of, 66–67
as social hot spot, 67, 70,
73, 76, 78
Famous for Fifteen Minutes,
76
Ferus Gallery, 44, 61, 63

"15 Drawings Based on the Writing of Truman Capote," 29

Film Culture, 69

Film Culture Award, 68–69, 78

Fitzpatrick, Joseph, 9–10

Flesh, 110–111

Flower Series, 77–78, 82, 84

**** *(Four Stars),* 97

Frankenstein, 119

Fredericks, Tina, 23–24

Gabor, Zsa Zsa, 34

Gagosian Gallery, 128

Geldzahler, Henry, 41, 49, 58–59, 67, 77, 89, 90

Giorno, John, 60–61

Girls of the Year, 75, 87, 95

Girman, Margie, 6, 13

Glamour, 23–24

Gold Marilyn Monroe, 51, 70

Grateful Dead, 89

Great Depression, 4, 19

Green, Sam, 83, 84

Green Burning Car 1, 58

Hackett, Pat, 76, 105, 109, 112, 123, 128, 130, 131

Hammer & Sickle Series, 122–123

Haring, Keith, 126

Harper's Bazaar, 22

Hayes, Ed, 134, 136

Heat, 118–119

Hendrix, Jimi, 91, 94

Herko, Freddie, 77, 78

Hickey, Dave, 77

Holzer, Baby Jane, 74–75, 81, 87, 135

Homosexual Action Movies, 83

homosexuality, 13–14, 20, 25–26, 31, 33–35, 47, 59, 66

Hompertz, Tom, 98

Hopper, Dennis, 62, 63, 75

Hughes, Fred, 96–97, 98, 101–102, 103, 105, 109, 111, 113, 116, 119, 122, 131, 134, 135, 136

Hugo Gallery, 29

Hyde, Russell, 17

I, a Man, 100

I. Miller ads, 30

Indiana, Robert, 40–41, 68

Institute of Contemporary Art (Boston), 94

Institute of Contemporary
    Art (Philadelphia), 83
International Velvet, 103
Interview, 107–110,
    111–112, 113, 116,
    127, 129, 131, 134
Iolas, Alexandre, 29

Jagger, Mick, 94. *see also*
    Rolling Stones
Johns, Jasper, 35, 36, 37,
    53
Johnson, Jed, 97–98, 101,
    103, 104, 109, 114,
    115, 116, 119, 129
Johnson, Philip, 51, 70
Joplin, Janis, 91

Karp, Ivan, 37–38, 39–40,
    41, 44, 78, 83, 103
Kennedy, Jackie, 47, 64,
    78, 116
Kennedy, John,
    assassination of, 64
Kennedy, Robert,
    assassination of, 104
King, Martin Luther, Jr., 57
Kish, Nick, 9, 13, 15

L'Amour, 119
Last Supper Series,
    131–132, 137

Latow, Muriel, 41–42
Leland, Ken, 132
Lennon, John, death of,
    135
Leo Castelli Gallery, 37, 53,
    78, 89, 96. *see also*
    Castelli, Leo
Lichtenstein, Roy, 38, 40,
    44, 45, 52
Life, 34, 57, 81
Lisanby, Charles, 33
Lonesome Cowboys,
    98–99, 110

Madonna, 126
Malanga, Gerard, 61–62,
    63–64, 73, 75, 83, 85,
    87, 88, 92, 103, 108,
    109, 135
  as assistant to Warhol,
    55–57, 77
Mao Zedong, 116–117
Marcos, Imelda, 113
Max's Kansas City,
    93–94
McCarthy hearings, 26
McGovern, George, 118
Mead, Taylor, 61, 63
Mekas, Jonas, 69
Mercedes-Benz, 130
Midgette, Alan, 96
Midnight Cowboy, 101

Miles, Sylvia, 118
Minnelli, Liza, 113, 135
Modern Photography, 77
Mona Lisa, 55
Monroe, Marilyn, 46–47, 49,
    50, 53, 78, 103, 116,
    117, 137
Morrissey, Paul, 82–83,
    84–85, 91–92, 94, 95,
    98, 101, 107–108, 109,
    110–111, 118, 119
Most Wanted Men Series,
    70, 78
Musée Galliera, 117
Museum of Contemporary
    Art, 137
Museum of Modern Art, 34,
    44, 51, 137
My Hustler, 83

Name, Billy, 66–67, 73, 74,
    77, 78, 85, 101, 102,
    105–106
New Museum, 138
New York, 116
New York Post, 133
New York Society of Clinical
    Psychologists, 87–88
New York Times, 116, 128,
    133
Nico, 87, 92, 103, 115
Nixon, Richard, 118

Normale, 83

O'Brien, Glenn, 116
Oldenburg, Claes, 40, 62,
    63
Ondine, 73–74, 78–79, 85,
    88, 92, 105
*129 Die in Jet (Plane
    Crash),* 49, 56
Ono, Yoko, 135
Oxidation paintings, 128

Paintings for Children,
    130
Participatory Art, 90
Pasadena Museum, 62
Pearlstein, Philip, 17, 18,
    21, 22, 23, 24, 25, 34
People, 110
Philips, Lisa, 137–138
*Philosophy of Andy Warhol:
    From A to B and Back
    Again, The,* 121
Picasso, Pablo, 137
Pivar, Stuart, 129
Pollock, Jackson, 35, 53
Poor Little Rich Girl, 81
Pop Art, 44, 45, 47, 49, 52,
    62, 63, 67, 68, 71, 75,
    126–127, 132, 137,
    138
    development of, 41, 53

189

Powell, Paige, 127, 131, 134

Presley, Elvis, 46, 47, 50, 52, 61, 63

Race Riot, 57

Rauschenberg, Robert, 35–36, 37, 38, 53, 54, 93

Reed, Lou, 87. *see also* Velvet Underground

Richardson, John, 135

Rockefeller, Nelson, 70

Rolling Stone, 108

Rolling Stones, 89, 116

Rose, Barbara, 116

Rosenquist, James, 40, 75

Rotten Rita, 74

Rubin, Barbara, 87

Ruskin, Mickey, 94

Russell, John, 133

St. Patrick's Cathedral, 135

St. Vitus' dance, 7, 11, 12

Scharf, Kenny, 126

Schnabel, Julian, 126

Screen Tests, 75–76

Screw, 108

Scull, Robert and Ethel, 54–55, 70, 71, 130

Sedgwick, Edie, 80–84, 85, 87

Segal, George, 47

Self-Portraits, 94, 97, 130, 137

Serbin, Mina, 6, 13

Serendipity 3, 32–33

Shadows, 123–124

Shot Blue Marilyn, 78–79

Shot Red Marilyn, 78–79

silk-screening process, 45, 46, 55

Silver George, 74

Sischy, Ingrid, 63, 128

skull paintings, 123

Snow, Carmel, 22

Solanas, Valerie, 100–102, 103, 104, 105, 111

Sonnabend Gallery, 82

Sotheby's, 136

Stable Gallery, 50, 70, 71

Stanley the Turtle, 74

Sticky Fingers, 116

Superstar, Ingrid, 74, 88

Superstars, 74, 83, 88, 91, 96, 103, 110, 115, 137

Tanager Gallery, 34

Tarzan and Jane Regained . . . Sort of, 63

Taylor, Elizabeth, 55

Temple, Shirley, 1–2, 14, 32, 81

Thirteen Most Wanted Men, The, 70

Time, 44, 53, 81, 93, 99, 103–104

Time Capsules, 122

Tony Shafrazi Gallery, 128

Torsos, 123

Trash, 111

25 Cats Name Sam and One Blue Pussy, 30

two-dollar-bill paintings, 50

Ultra Violet, 74, 76, 81–82, 103, 115

University of Pittsburgh, 14–15

Velvet Underground, 86–89, 121

Vietnam War, 57

Village Voice, 88

Vinyl, 81

Viva (aka Viva!), 95, 98, 99, 101, 103, 105, 108, 115, 118

Vogue, 81

Vollmer, Larry, 20

Ward, Eleanor, 50, 51, 58, 71

Warhol, Andy. *see also*
names of individual pieces

art ambitions of, 34, 36, 39, 41, 44

auction of possessions of, 136

birth and childhood of, 1–3, 6–10

choice of subjects by, 36, 41, 44, 46, 48–49, 64

in college, 14–21

commercial art of, 19–20, 22–24, 25, 29–30, 34, 36, 38, 39, 41, 45, 129–130, 135–136, 137

critics' response to work by, 44, 52–53, 58, 63, 64, 69, 71, 78, 83, 93, 99, 116, 118, 123, 128, 133

death and funeral of, 132–133, 134–135

death as theme in art of, 47, 49, 57, 124

depression and panic attacks of, 41

diary of, 105, 130, 131

filmmaking of, 60–61, 63, 67–69, 75–76, 81, 82–83, 84–85, 91–93, 94, 96, 97–99, 100, 110–111, 118–119

191

finances of, 89, 96, 111

in high school, 12–14

image repetition in art by, 44, 47, 54

lectures by, 87–88, 95–96

legacy of, 127, 135–138

love of films of, 6–7, 14, 21, 60

mass production in art of, 45, 46, 49

name change of, 24

politics in art by, 57–59, 122–123

portraits by, 49, 112–113, 122, 127, 129, 137. see also names of individual subjects

public response to work by, 50–51, 53, 68, 69, 71, 93, 94

religiousness of, 3, 132, 135

retrospective exhibitions of work by, 115, 137

sexuality of, 13–14, 20, 25–26, 31, 33–35, 47, 60, 66, 97–98, 114, 129

shooting of, 101–104, 120, 124

travels of, 33, 62

Warhola, Andrej (father), 2, 3–6, 8

death of, 11–12

Warhola, Andrew. see Warhol, Andy

Warhola, John (brother), 2–3, 5, 6–7, 8, 12, 14, 28, 41, 48, 58, 104, 118, 134–135

Warhola, Julia (mother), 2, 3–4, 5–6, 12, 29, 30, 34, 41, 47–48, 62, 103, 104, 114

artwork by, 32

as caretaker of Andy, 2, 6–8, 11, 18, 28–29, 32

death of, 118

illnesses of, 14, 96, 115

Warhola, Paul (brother), 2, 6, 7, 8, 12, 17–18, 41, 48, 58, 104, 118, 134–135

Whitney Museum, 115–116

Why Pick on Me, 21

Wild Raspberries, 30

Willers, Carl, 31

Wolfe, Tom, 88

Wood, Natalie, 46

Woodlawn, Holly, 111, 118

World War I, 5–6

World War II, 12, 16

World's Fair, 70

about the authors

Jan Greenberg and Sandra Jordan are the authors of numerous acclaimed books about art, including *Vincent van Gogh: Portrait of an Artist,* which was named a Robert F. Sibert Honor Book and an ALA Notable Book; *Action Jackson*, also a Robert F. Sibert Honor Book and an ALA Notable Book; *Runaway Girl: The Artist Louise Bourgeois*, a *School Library Journal* Best Book; and *Chuck Close Up Close*, recipient of a *Boston Globe–Horn Book* Honor, winner of the Norman A. Sugarman Biography Award, and an ALA Notable Book. Jan Greenberg, the author of many noteworthy books for young readers as well as a teacher and art educator, lives in St. Louis. Sandra Jordan, an editor and photographer as well as a writer, lives in New York.